praise for

Fast Feng Shui:
9 Simple Principles for Transforming Your Life by Energizing Your Home

"*Fast Feng Shui* is a delightful book and filled with great tips and lots of positive affirmations. It is good for beginners and for advanced students. You can open it at any page and find useful information. I love this book!"

— LOUISE L. HAY
author, *You Can Heal Your Life*
and *Empowering Women*

"In the often complex world of feng shui, *Fast Feng Shui* is a breath of fresh air. Stephanie Roberts takes ancient concepts and makes them applicable to modern life in a way that is fun, valuable, and fast."

— DENISE LINN
author, *Feng Shui for the Soul*,
Sacred Space, and *Space Clearing*

"Creatively integrates your personality type and the power of intention with the basics of Western Feng Shui."

— JAMI LIN
internationally renowned Feng Shui expert,
instructor, and author

"Finally, a fun and easy-to-understand feng shui book that is logical, coherent, and user friendly.... I highly recommend this book to beginners as well as seasoned practitioners."

— ROBIN LENNON
author, *Home Design from the Inside Out*

"*Fast Feng Shui* is a fabulous, fun, smart, effective way to empower yourself and your environment and begin to attract and create the life you really want. It makes the mystical easy and accessible. Stephanie Roberts is brilliant!"

— SONIA CHOQUETTE, PhD
author, *Your Heart's Desire*, *True Balance*,
and *The Psychic Pathway*

also by Stephanie Roberts:

Fast Feng Shui: 9 Simple Principles for Transforming Your Life by Energizing Your Home

and, coming soon:

Fast Feng Shui for Prosperity: Living an Abundant Life

Fast Feng Shui for Newlyweds: Creating Balance and Harmony for Your Life Together

Fast Feng Shui for Singles

108 Ways to Heal Your Home and Attract Romance

STEPHANIE ROBERTS

LOTUS·POND·PRESS

Kahului, HI

Published by Lotus Pond Press, 415 Dairy Road #E-144, Kahului, HI, 96732
www.lotuspondpress.com

"Fast Feng Shui" is a trademark of Lotus Pond Press

Cover design by Dunn + Associates; author photo by Diana Kassir

Publisher's Cataloging-in-Publication Data
(provided by Quality Books, Inc.)

Roberts, Stephanie, 1958-
    Fast feng shui for singles : 108 ways to heal your home and attract
romance / Stephanie Roberts. -- 1st ed.
    p. cm. -- (Fast feng shui series)
    Includes index.
    LCCN: 2001117702
    ISBN: 1-931383-04-9

    1. Feng shui. 2. Love--Misscellanea. 3. Man-woman relationships
--Miscellanea. I. Title.

BF1779.F4R63 2001   133.3'337
                               QB101-200631

printed in the United States of America
10 9 8 7 6 5 4 3 2 1

dedicated to
all my ex-loves with
whom things didn't work out.
I couldn't have written this
book without you!

Author's Note

This book is for all of you who want more love and romance in your lives. You know someone wonderful is out there for you, but aren't sure where or how to find that future partner. Now you can use the power of contemporary Western feng shui to transform your home and your heart into environments that welcome romance and support a lasting, loving relationship with the man or woman of your dreams.

Those who have read the first Fast Feng Shui book have learned the power of feng shui as a tool for self-discovery and personal growth. With this new book, you can harness that power to heal your home and attract romance, just like I did.

Fast Feng Shui for Singles draws on my personal experience, both as a feng shui consultant and as a single person looking for romance. I learned the hard way that the feng shui techniques I'd been told were effective didn't work so well if I wasn't emotionally ready for what I thought I wanted. It was only when I stopped trying so hard to find a partner, and shifted my focus to using feng shui to resolve past relationship issues and clear the energy of my home, that I was able to create the inner foundation for meeting someone new.

A cornerstone of the Fast Feng Shui philosophy is that you will get better results with feng shui, in faster time, when you focus on specific goals and target your activities to what you really need. *Fast Feng Shui for Singles* presents an entirely new and unique approach to using feng shui for love and romance, by tailoring your strategies to the specific needs and challenges of each of the five phases of the Fast Feng Shui Relationship Cycle.

It starts with helping you to heal the heartache caused by the failed relationships of the past, and shows you how to clear your home of old, stale relationship energy before you try to attract a new romantic partner. You'll learn feng shui tips and techniques to help you through the dating game, as well as ways to nurture and support a budding relationship once you connect with someone special.

Along the way, you'll find lots of journaling exercises, meditations, and rituals for healing your home and heart, jump-starting your social life, and removing barriers to intimacy, communication, and commitment.

In fact, there are far more than the promised 108 tips in these pages. I decided to keep that number in the title because it is an important feng shui power number, and reflects my intention to help you powerfully transform your love life and connect with your perfect partner!

Wishing you peace, love and joy,

Stephanie R.

PS—If you're on-line, be sure to visit www.fastfengshui.com for lots more feng shui information and links to a wide range of feng shui and other useful sites.

Table of Contents

Appendices

How to Get Cupid on Your Side

Feng Shui and Your Love Life

FENG SHUI (say "fung shway") is an ancient Chinese practice that aims to maximize the beneficial movement of *chi*—the life force present in all things—through your home. *Feng shui* means "wind and water." Just as fresh air, clean water, and organic foods nourish our physical bodies, so does fresh, clean *chi* nourish our lives.

Chi wants to meander through your home like a gentle breeze or a winding stream. Where the flow of *chi* in your home is blocked or weak, it becomes like a pond choked with algae and fallen leaves. You may feel tired, depressed, unable to focus, hampered in your efforts to move forward in your life and connect with a potential partner.

Where *chi* flows too strongly, it is like a hurricane or flood. You may feel out of control, overly emotional, or anxious much of the time. Communication becomes more difficult, and relationships can feel unstable as you struggle to "keep your head above water" through what may seem like an endless string of bad luck.

Feng shui uses shape, color, texture, sound, light, symbolic imagery and the arrangement of your furniture to adjust the energy of your home. Positive influences are encouraged and enhanced, while negative factors are corrected. The goal is to create an attractive, safe, and nurturing space where you can live in comfort and more effectively and successfully pursue your goals for a fulfilling love life.

A key principle of contemporary Western feng shui* is that certain areas of your home have a strong impact on specific aspects of your life. When the areas of your home affecting your love life are cluttered, stagnant, or missing from your floor plan, it can be difficult to attract and maintain a good relationship. Other feng shui problems that may affect relationships include *sha* (negative) *chi* such as an exposed beam directly over your bed.

Poor feng shui in your home can also lead to increased arguments and miscommunication, affect your reputation, impair your ability to meet new people, and hinder your personal growth—all of which can contribute to difficulties in your love life.

A key principle of feng shui is that everything is connected energetically. Your thoughts and feelings, even your behavior, can be influenced by your surroundings, while the state of your home is a reflection of your mood and attitude.

A dark, dingy, and untidy bedroom, for example, contributes to an atmosphere of fatigue and depression, which in turn makes it harder for you to find the energy to clean the place up and air it out. In feng shui terms, it is also undermining your ability to attract and maintain a joyful and supportive romantic attachment.

Feng shui gives you insight and incentive to become a mindful caretaker of your home. As a result, you live in greater harmony with your surroundings, which can better support you in achieving what you desire—in your love relationships and in all other aspects of your life.

---

* For more information on the differences between classical Chinese feng shui and the modern, Western version of feng shui, see the *Fast Feng Shui* book or visit www.fastfengshui.com.

The Fast Feng Shui™ Approach

The Fast Feng Shui Series is designed for everyone who would like to get started with feng shui, or apply basic feng shui principles to a specific aspect of life. It provides an approach to contemporary Western feng shui that is easy to learn and simple to follow, and helps you figure out what changes *you* need to make in *your* home to address the issues that most concern you right now.

Fast Feng Shui is based on the idea that you will see better results, more quickly, when your feng shui efforts are targeted to specific personal goals and when you put the full power of your intention into the changes that you make to your home. It focuses on adjustments you can make right away, without remodeling or renovations, and helps you target the specific areas of your home that will have the biggest impact on your key issues.

Although *Fast Feng Shui for Singles* follows the contemporary Western practice of aligning the *ba gua* energy map to the main doorway of a space, it accommodates the compass orientation as well. You'll explore these energetic nuances of your floor plan as you learn to locate your relationship power spots.

The affirmations and visualizations used to empower your changes are an important ingredient to your success with Fast Feng Shui. I also recommend keeping a feng shui journal, so you can explore your emotional reactions to the work and grow through your experiences.

I believe that feng shui should empower you as well as your home, and I encourage you to be creative and playful as you use feng shui to transform your home and your love life.

What to Expect from Feng Shui

Traditionally, feng shui is seen as one of five factors that influence a person's life. In addition to feng shui, the other factors are your karma, luck, education, and actions, each of which may also contribute to the past, present, and future state of your love life.

- **Karma**: your destiny or fate; the big picture of your life—whether you were born rich or poor, healthy or disabled, the major challenges you face during your life. Some relationship problems you encounter may be attributable in part to your karma, especially if there are significant life lessons to be gained from the experience.

- **Luck**: your astrology; periods of good or bad fortune; the types of situations and opportunities that come your way. Some people are lucky in love—as in other aspects of life—and others are not. Feng shui can help you make the most of a period of good luck, and can help you weather bad times more smoothly.

- **Education**: your formal education as well as things that you do to better yourself, including therapy. For many people, attracting and maintaining a successful romantic relationship involves dealing with issues of trust, intimacy, and commitment. Feng shui can assist you in gaining the most insight and benefit from work with a therapist. Therapy can also help make your feng shui efforts more effective by helping you to recognize and overcome inner resistance and self-sabotaging behavior patterns.

- **Actions**: the integrity of your conduct; doing good deeds; taking care of yourself. The golden rule of doing unto others as you would have them do unto you applies in feng shui as in all other things. Always use feng shui with the intention that it result in the best possible outcome for all concerned; feng shui should never be used to control or manipulate others. Feng shui can help you attract new potential partners into your life, but responding appropriately to those new romantic opportunities is up to you.

The impact of feng shui is most immediate when the difficulties you are experiencing are caused by poor feng shui in the first place, rather than by your karma, astrology, or actions. When this is the case, correcting the problem can have dramatic and quick results. Expect your social life to heat up, your phone to start ringing more often, and for "likely prospects" to turn up just about everywhere you go.

When other life factors are involved, feng shui can help you gain the perspective and insight necessary for getting your love life back on track. You are likely to see improvements in your energy, enthusiasm and ability to communicate productively with others—all of which will have a dramatic influence on your romantic life in the long run.

One of the most effective ways to approach feng shui is with the goal of enhancing your personal growth and development. Those who turn to feng shui for a quick fix for emotional problems often discover that it brings them lots of opportunities to repeat their old patterns of behavior! If you have trouble sustaining a long-term relationship because of intimacy issues, for example, using feng shui to attract a new relationship may bring someone new into your life. And then there you will be, faced with the same old hang-ups.

If you are really committed to changing your life, feng shui can be a powerful ally on your journey of self-discovery and healing. In fact, feng shui is likely to bring you situations and opportunities that will help you overcome the challenges you most need to address in your quest for personal growth and fulfillment.

The effects of feng shui can be sudden and dramatic or they might be gradual and subtle. There is no way of predicting exactly what will manifest for you, when, or how. Approach feng shui as an adventure, and be open to the unanticipated outcome that ends up taking you exactly where you need to go. For those who are ready and willing to change, a dramatic and fulfilling shift in your love life really is possible.

The Power of Your Intention

On an energetic level, you are intricately connected to everything in your home. This means that the strength of your intention to change your life is an integral part of the success of your feng shui cures, and that feng shui will work best for you when you focus on what you really want to change in your life.

If you make generic feng shui adjustments without targeting them to your personal issues and goals, you will not have a strong emotional involvement in what you are doing. Without emotional investment in the work, it is difficult to trigger significant changes in your life.

Your thoughts are remarkably powerful. Think of the difference in your own energy when you are excited about something, compared to times when you feel lonely, unhappy, or depressed. When you constantly dwell on how dissatisfied you are with a life situation, your energy becomes stuck there. As you feng shui your home to enhance your love life, it is important to support your actions with an attitude of enthusiasm and anticipation. Apply feng shui with confidence, optimism, and a sense of adventure. This will keep you motivated, and will help to activate the energy of your home.

Empowering Your Feng Shui Changes

Using the combined power of your body, speech, and mind to activate and reinforce the changes you are making to your home is a key ingredient in successful feng shui. The empowerment process presented here greatly enhances your efforts by focusing the power of your mind on what you are doing. When you focus your mind on your reasons for making a feng shui adjustment and on what you hope to achieve as a result, your feng shui will be much more effective.

Traditionally, after making your feng shui adjustments, you use the "dispelling mudra"* nine times while repeating the mantra, *om mani padme hum*, nine times. The *mudra*, or hand gesture, represents the power of body; the *mantra* is the power of speech, and visualizing your desired outcome while you use the *mantra* and *mudra* is the power of mind.

Many clients have said they feel silly chanting in Sanskrit while flicking their fingers in the air. In response to their requests for a more comfortable method, I developed the following alternative approach:

1. **Keep your focus**: Practice mindful awareness while you are making feng shui changes, so that your physical actions have power and intent behind them. This is the "body" reinforcement.

---

* To make the dispelling mudra, point your index and pinky fingers straight out while curling your middle and ring finger toward the palm and holding them in place with your thumb. (Women, use your right hand; men use your left hand.) Now flick the middle and ring finger out. This dispells any negative energy from whatever you have flicked at.

2. **State your intention**: After you have made your adjustment, make a verbal affirmation that clearly states the intended shift in your energy and/or circumstances. You can say this out loud, whisper it softly to yourself, or even express it subvocally. This is the "speech" reinforcement.

3. **Visualize your desired outcome**: Following your affirmation, visualize your desired outcome in your mind, as if it has already taken place. Make your visualization as specific and concrete as possible, using all of your senses, so that you experience the feeling of joy, satisfaction, or relief that your desired results will bring. This is the "mind" reinforcement.

If you feel inspired to close your empowerment by saying "Let it be done," or "May the blessings be," or any similar phrase, you may certainly do so. Of course, you may also use the dispelling mudra and mantra method, or you may combine those elements from both methods that are comfortable for you.

You can repeat the affirmation and visualization steps daily for three, nine, or 27 days for even stronger effect. This is an excellent way to maintain your focus over time, and to help shift both your own energy and the energy of your home. If you decide to do this, it's okay to vary the affirmations and visualizations that you use— you're sure to think of new details as you go along.

AFFIRMATIONS

Phrase your affirmations in the present tense. Saying something "will" happen implies that it will take place in the future—which means you will never experience it in the present. Use "now" or whatever phrase will put your affirmation into the present. Instead of, "I *will* open myself to experience true love and intimacy," say, "I *now* open myself to experience true love and intimacy."

VISUALIZATION

Visualization involves both seeing a desired change in your mind's eye and feeling the joy and satisfaction of having achieved your desires. You know you are *feeling* the desired change if there's a smile on your face and your heart feels light and expansive. If you're not smiling, and your body feels tight and heavy, you are still feeling lack and want. It is important to achieve this emotional shift to a feeling of joy and celebration. Don't be discouraged if it's not easy to feel the shift at first. It will come with practice.

TIMING

During the hours of 11 AM to 1 PM, and 11 PM TO 1 AM, the energy of the day is shifting; these are good times to empower feng shui changes. If these hours are inconvenient, find a time when you will be calm, alert, and focused.

Those who work with Chinese or western astrology can use either system to choose an auspicious day and/or time to empower your changes. Other dates that have strong personal significance for you (such as your birthday or an important anniversary) can also be good times to perform empowerments.

--- *Note* ---

Two excellent books about using the power of your mind and emotions to create change are Shakti Gawain's classic, Creative Visualization, *and* Excuse Me, Your Life is Waiting, *by Lynn Grabhorn. See the Resources pages in the back of this book for more information.*

How to Use This Book

Before we jump into exploring the Fast Feng Shui Relationship Cycle and making changes to your home, you should be familiar with the basic tools of feng shui. These include the *ba gua* energy map, which determines what areas of your home are most affecting your love life, and the five feng shui elements—key influences that help you balance and correct the *chi* of your home to encourage love and romance.

For those who are new to feng shui (and for anyone who could use a refresher), an introduction to the *ba gua* and the five elements is included in the Appendices at the back of the book. It would be a good idea for you to read through that basic information before moving ahead to the next chapter, which provides a brief summary of the nine guiding principles taught in the first Fast Feng Shui book.

The rest of this book takes you step by step through the five stages of the Relationship Cycle. At each stage, we will explore how to work with the *ba gua* energy map and the five elements to make appropriate adjustments to your home, based on the objectives and tasks for that stage.

While you may jump ahead to read about the phase you are in right now, it's also a good idea to review the chapters on earlier stages of the Relationship Cycle, to make sure you don't overlook any feng shui tips that might be helpful for you.

Keep a Feng Shui Journal

I highly recomment that you use a notebook or journal to write down your feng shui goals, actions, and results. You can use your notebook to:

- Record your answers to the questions about your experiences and attitudes that you will find throughout this book

- Make a list of potential changes you could make to your home, so you can more easily prioritize your feng shui tasks and track your progress

- Write down the affirmations and visualizations you will use to empower your feng shui changes

- Record the specific changes you make to your home, including when and why you made them

- Keep track of the changes you experience in your love life as you feng shui your home

- Explore any emotional issues that come up for you as a result of your feng shui work

Your notebook doesn't have to be fancy, but it should be new so it has clean energy. It should be small enough so it is easy to carry around, yet large enough to write and sketch in easily. Good sizes are 5"x7" or 6"x9".

Be prepared to really use your notebook: stuff things in it, tear pages out, be creative. As soon as you start changing things around in your home, your own energy will start to shift as well. When you do feng shui, you are likely to find yourself more creative in all aspects of life, seeing things from new angles and having new ideas. Write them all down!

Getting Ready

You will want to have several copies of your floor plan available as you work on your home. If your home has more than one storey, you'll want a separate page for each floor. It's also helpful, if you live in a house with a yard, to have a map of your entire property at hand.

If you don't have a floor plan available, it's not difficult to draw one up. I'll tell you how in a moment. First, though, I'd like you to get a blank, unlined piece of paper and sketch the layout of your home *by hand and from memory*. Don't obsess over making it perfect, and please *don't* refer to a floor plan if you already have one, and don't use a tapemeasure or ruler to measure anything before you draw. Your hand-drawn sketch should include the front door, hallways, and major rooms: living room, kitchen, bedrooms, bathrooms, etc. Show the location of windows, doors, closets. You don't need to draw your furniture: I just want a basic layout of your home.

Done? Great. Set it aside (we'll come back to it in a moment) and get out your accurate floor plan. If you don't have one of those, you will need: a pad of graph paper (1/4" grid is a good size), a pencil and eraser, a tape measure to measure your space, a ruler to make drawing straight lines easier, and a roll of tape for taping pieces of paper together.

Decide what scale you are going to use: if you are using 1/4" grid paper, you could say that one little square will equal half a foot (6") when you measure a room.

Decide where to start. A corner room is good. Measure the length and width of the room, convert inches or feet into squares on your graph paper, and draw the outline of that room on your paper. Add the door, and mark where the windows are.

Go to whatever room or hallway is next to the one you started with, and measure that one with your tape measure. Convert inches and feet into little squares on your paper, and outline that space. Add doors and windows, and move on.

Unless you are very left-brain oriented and have planned carefully, you will sooner or later run out of space on your sheet of graph paper. That's okay. Tape a fresh piece of paper to the one you started with, and keep going.

If you have a large home and have created an unwieldy mess of taped-together papers—and have not yet run out of patience— you can make a cleaner, neater version at a smaller scale. Using your first draft as a guide, redraw your layout, making each little square on your graph paper equal to a greater measure this time. For example, if your first version had a 1/4" square equal to 6" in real measure, you could now use a 1/4" square to equal one or two feet, or whatever scale is most useful for you.

If you can get the entire outline of your home down to under 11"x17", that's great, because any good copy shop will be able to duplicate that size for you. If your home is not particularly grand, you can probably get a basic outline onto a standard 8-1/2"x11" or legal size (8-1/2"x14") piece of paper.

Now you are ready to have a bunch of photocopies made. Be sure to keep one copy clean and unmarked, in case you need to make more duplicates later.

Before we go on, I'd also like you to take out that hand-drawn floor plan I asked you to do, and compare it to the accurate "I-measured-everything" version. Did you get anything glaringly wrong when you sketched your home from memory? Most people do, so don't feel bad! Take a look at what you misrepresented, and think about what your subconscious might be telling you.

For example, I have several single clients whose free-hand house plans show a bedroom that is significantly smaller than it really is. One client drew her bedroom the right size, but forgot to add the door—there was no way to get in. Another drew the hallway to the bedroom as narrow bottleneck, and someone else drew a closet that was almost as big as the bedroom (and boy, was there a lot of clutter lurking in there!)

Bedrooms aren't the only aspect of a floor plan that can get messed up. Did your front door end up in the right place, or did it wander into a different *gua*? Did you draw an extension or a missing area* way out of scale? If so, what rooms or *guas* are affected?

Anything that jumps out at you as a major goof is a sign of imbalance in the *chi* of that space. It may also indicate a subconsious issue you have with the aspects of your life that are related to that space. If you want a relationship, but forgot to draw a door to your bedroom, are you really ready to welcome someone into your life? If your kitchen ended up half the size it should be, does a craving for emotional nourishment make you too needy when you fall in love?

These interpretations are extremely personal, so a similar goof on two people's floor plans could mean very different things. Trust your intuition, or take your floorplans with you next time you go see your shrink, and keep these clues in mind as we feng shui your love life.

Great, you're ready to begin. Let's start with a quick review of the basic Fast Feng Shui Principles—which includes finding out which areas of your home are your relationship "power spots," so you can mark those on your floor plan.

---

* If you don't know what these are, read pages 190-191. It's an important concept for evaluating your floor plan and power spots.

Guiding Principles

Note

If you've read *Fast Feng Shui: 9 Simple Principles for Transforming Your Life by Energizing Your Home,* you're already familiar with the key concepts in this chapter. The review presented here takes another look at these basic guidelines from the perspective of applying them to your love life. New readers, spend some time with this chapter, so you can keep these principles in mind as you feng shui your home to enhance romance.

Principle 1:
Know What You Want

Having specific goals for what you are looking for in a romantic partner will help you to focus your feng shui efforts and to define the affirmations and visualizations that you will use to empower your changes. You may find that you have both short- and long-term goals for how you want to change your love life. For example, you may want to meet someone interesting today, but that doesn't mean you'll be ready to say "I do" tomorrow—even if marriage is an important long-term goal for you.

JOURNALING

The nine areas of the *ba gua* provide a useful framework for exploring relationship goals. Here are some questions that you can ask yourself, based on the life aspirations defined by the *ba gua*. Refer to the *ba gua* chart on page 188 for additional meanings to explore.

- *Kun* (relationships)

  How important is marriage, in both the long and short term?

  How do you want to be treated in a relationship?

- *Dui* (children and creativity)

  How important are childen, and what are the specific issues involved (such as, if you already have kids or have a strong desire to have or not have a baby)?

  How would you feel about getting involved with someone who already has children of his or her own?

  How important is creativity to you? What time, space, or financial resources do you need for your creative work?

- *Chien* (helpful friends and travel)

  What kind of support will you need from your partner?

  What, if anything, could you not be supportive of?

  Will frequent travel by you or your partner be a problem?

  Are you open to a long-distance romance?

  Are you willing to relocate for love? To where, or how far?

- *Kan* (career)

  Will getting involved in a serious relationship affect your career, and if so, how?

  What career compromises are you willing (or not) to make in order to sustain a successful relationship?

- *Ken* (self-understanding, knowledge, spirituality)

  How important is a shared religious background or practice?

  If you have or want children, how do you plan to raise them?

  Do you have plans for future education, such as graduate studies, that might affect a relationship?

- *Jen* (family)

  What, if any, family issues might impact a future relationship, and in what ways?

- *Hsun* (wealth)

  How important is it to you to find a partner who is financially successful or independent?

  What expectations do you have about shared or divided financial responsibility?

  Do you have any personal money issues, such as a large debt, that could impact a future relationship?

- *Li* (fame and reputation)

  How do you want others to perceive your relationship?

  What words would they use to describe it?

Principle 2:
Locate Your Power Spots

POWER SPOTS are the areas of your home where feng shui will have the most direct impact on the aspects of your life that you wish to change. By focusing your feng shui energy and activity on these areas, you increase your chances of success.

The location of your power spots depends on the specific layout of your home. When using feng shui to enhance your love life, *kun gua* (the relationships area of the *ba gua*) is an important power spot wherever it occurs in your home.

When you align the *ba gua* with the main entry to a space, *kun gua* (relationships) is always the area in the back right corner:

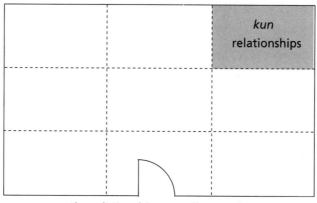

the relationships area (*kun gua*)
is the far right corner of a space

Get out your floor plan, and your property map if you have one, and follow the steps below to locate your relationship power spots. (Review page 189 if you aren't sure how to place the *ba gua*.)

1. Where is *kun gua* on your property? (Place the lower edge of the *ba gua* along the street in front of your house.) Draw a circle around this area; it is a relationship power spot.

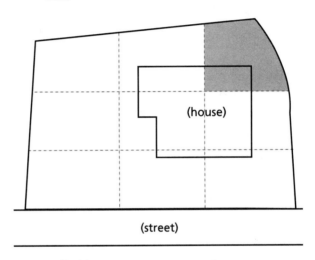

find *kun gua* on your property

2. Using the floor plan of your house or apartment, place the *ba gua* over the entire main floor, aligning it with the front door. What part of your home is in *kun gua?* Draw a circle around that area; it is one of your relationship power spots. Don't panic if your home is "missing" that far right corner. You'll learn what to do about that later in the book.

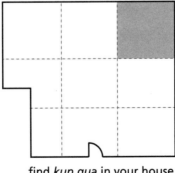

find *kun gua* in your house

3. Now place the *ba gua* over the room you circled in step 2.
    Align the *ba gua* with the door to that space—it might be
    rotated one way or the other compared to the rest of the
    house. Where is *kun gua* within that one room? Mark that
    corner of the room; it is an important relationship power
    spot.

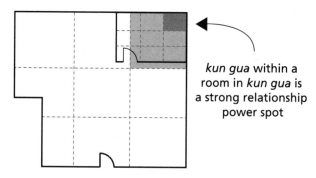

kun gua within a
room in *kun gua* is
a strong relationship
power spot

If you look back at the property *ba gua* on the previous page,
you'll see that this area of this room of this house is also in
kun gua of the property. This multi-layered effect makes it a
very powerful relationship power spot.

4. Place the *ba gua* over your bedroom, (turn it if necessary to
    line up with the doorway) and locate *kun gua*. This is your
    most important power spot, regardless of its location in the
    home, because your energetic connection is strongest to your
    personal space. We'll be working with the feng shui of your
    bedroom a lot throughout this book, and *kun gua* within the
    bedroom will get a lot of attention.

    Look to see where *kun gua* is in your living room and other
    important areas of the house. These areas are also relation-
    ship power spots—especially if they overlap with another
    power spot in some way.

5. When the *ba gua* is placed according to compass directions,
    kun gua (relationships) is in the southwest. If you know what
    direction your house faces (or can step outside to take a
    compass reading), it's worth taking a look to see what rooms
    are in the southwest sector of your home.

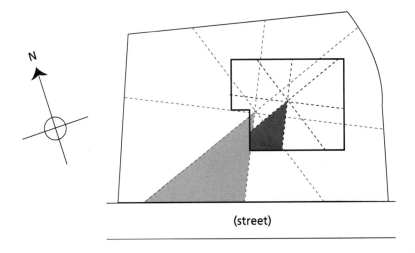

(street)

if you use a compass orientation for the *ba gua*,
kun gua is in the southwest

Note that with the compass directions, slicing a "pie" into
eight sectors is an easier way to divide the space than rotat-
ing a grid and trying to figure out where the boundaries
between the *guas* should be. The area around the point where
the lines come together is the *tai chi* (center), even though it is
not specifically defined by a sector line.

Are any of the relationship power spots you identified in the
previous steps also in the southwestern sector of your property, home, or a major room? If so, they will be even more
important areas on which to focus your feng shui efforts.

Other Areas of the Ba Gua

In addition to working on your relationship power spots, you may from time to time wish to include secondary areas in your feng shui practice, such as *chien gua* (helpful friends), *kan gua* (social contacts), *li gua* (reputation), and so on.

For example, perhaps you've recently gone through a difficult breakup, and recognize that a good therapist could help you work through some issues that have come up for you. If you need to find someone to work with, *chien gua* (helpful friends) might be important for you now. If you already have a therapist, but want to achieve greater insight and progress, perhaps *ken gua* (self-understanding) could use some feng shui attention.

Think about whether there is a specific area of the *ba gua* that you'd like to work with in addition to *kun gua* (relationships). If there is—and it's fine if there's not—repeat steps 1-5 on the preceding pages for this additional *gua*. (A different colored pen or pencil is helpful for this. You can also turn to page 194 to find out which compass direction is associated with your secondary *gua*.)

The purpose of this work is not to overload you with power spots, but to identify where your different power spots overlap. These will be especially important areas for you to pay attention to as you begin to feng shui your home.

Keep in mind also that your needs and focus will shift as you progress through the five phases of the Fast Feng Shui Relationship Cycle. As they do, some of your power spots may change as well. We'll revisit this layered approach to the *ba gua* and your power spots as we explore the different phases of the Relationship Cycle.

Principle 3:
Create a Path for Chi

One of the objectives of feng shui is to create a gentle, nurturing flow of *chi* through your home. When your primary intention is to rejuvenate your love life, you especially want to make sure that *chi* can get from your front door to your relationship power spots without being blocked or diverted along the way.

Your front door is called the "mouth of *chi*" because it is the primary way *chi* enters your home. If your mouth of *chi* has poor feng shui, the *chi* of your entire home will suffer, and you may find it difficult to recognize and respond to opportunities. (You'll learn more about the importance of doors and entryways in Phase 2 of the Relationship Cycle.)

Inside your home, *chi* likes to flow in gentle curves, and will exit through side doors and windows. Long straight corridors will funnel *chi* very quickly toward whatever is at the far end. Active spaces of your home should have a more active flow of *chi*. *Chi* should slow down and linger in the places you like to sit down and relax at the end of the day, or where you need to focus and concentrate on the work at hand.

Creating a path for *chi* involves getting rid of the stuff that piles up behind doors, moving furniture so it creates a smooth traffic flow through the home, and using cures such as mirrors, wind chimes and faceted crystal balls* to manage the flow of *chi*.

---

* See pages 205-212 in the Appendix for guidelines on using feng shui cures and objects.

Principle 4:
Repaint, Repair, Renew

One of the key principles of feng shui is that even minor problems in the home can have a major effect on your life. A well-kept home will always have better *chi* than one where maintenance tasks have been allowed to pile up. Some common problems to look out for are listed below, along with the effect they could be having on your life. While it's a good idea to correct these situations anywhere in your home, be sure to pay special attention to your relationship power spots.

- A cracked walkway, sagging porch steps, loose railings, or rotting threshold can all literally or symbolically trip you up and make it difficult to achieve your goals.

- Doors that are difficult to open make it difficult for you to progress in life. Sticky locks create the same kind of problem.

- Dirty windows cloud your judgment and make it hard to see things clearly. This can manifest as physical eye problems or symbolically as difficulty recognizing what's reallly going on.

- Broken or cracked windows are a sure sign of deteriorating *chi* in that part of the home, weakening whatever aspect of your life is affected by that *gua*.

- Dirty, cracked, or mottled mirrors can have a harmful effect— literally or symbolically—on whatever is reflected in them, including yourself and your self-perception.

- Burnt-out lights, fixtures that don't work, and inadequate lighting all contribute to a lack of vision, energy, and initiative in that *gua* and in the related area of your life.

- Plumbing problems indicate that resources are leaking away from the home.

Now that you know where your power spots are, it's a good idea to take a close look at those areas of your house. Make a note of any new or long-overdue housekeeping, maintenance, and repair tasks, and make getting them done as soon as possible a feng shui priority!

Principle 5:
Clean Up Your Clutter

Clutter in your home blocks the smooth flow of *chi* through your space, weighs you down energetically, and keeps you in the past. Clutter makes it very difficult to move ahead in your life.

When your relationship power spots are filled with clutter, your love live can feel stagnant, messy, moribund, or like a burden rather than a joy. You may find yourself living in the past emotionally, unable to let go of "what if" and "if only" thinking so you can focus on someone new. Spring cleaning your power spots is a great way to spring clean your love life and get new energy flowing.

An additional benefit of getting rid of your clutter is that it can literally lighten you up and help you lose weight! All that stuck energy in your environment affects you on a physical level, and encourages extra pounds to hang around. I'd heard about this, and discovered that it is true when I moved from New York City to Maui. I sold, gave away, or threw out most of my things, including a ten-year accumulation of clutter, and in the process I lost 12 pounds. If self-consciousness about your weight is contributing to a lack of energy for your love life, tackling your clutter everywhere in the house should be a key part of your romantic make-over plan.

We'll take a closer look at why—and how—to get rid of clutter as we explore Phase 2 of the Relationship Cycle.

Principle 6:
Neutralize Negative Influences

Dirt and clutter are obvious examples of *sha* (negative) *chi*, but other forms of negative energy could also be affecting your home and your love life. Many of these are not very obvious until you've learned what to look for. Several specific examples of *sha chi* are discussed in the chapter on Phase 4 of the Relationship Cycle, where we look at removing any causes of discord from your bedroom and the rest of the home.

You can begin the work of neutralizing harmful influences by examining each of your relationship power spots for "secret arrows" affecting any area where you eat, sleep, relax, or work. Secret arrows are caused when *chi* flows along a smooth wall or surface and comes to a sharp angle or corner. The turbulent energy created at the corner can result in stress, anxiety, difficult sleep, arguments, conflict, and so on.

"secret arrows" are *sha chi* caused by a sharp corner or angle

The sharp corner of a table, the edges of a shelf, even points or angles on a lighting fixture or piece of statuary can all cause a disruption in the smooth flow of *chi* nearby. The size and height of the angle will affect how strong the negative influence is. You can "cure" a sharp angle by shielding it with a large plant, a piece of fabric, or a faceted crystal ball. Hang the crystal from the ceiling with red string cut to a multiple of nine inches for best effect.

Principle 7:
Activate Your Power Spots

Activating your relationship power spots is the part of feng shui where you really get to use your creativity and have fun. There are lots of ways to bring positive, creative energy into your relationship power spots, including:

- Faceted crystal balls

- Bells and wind chimes

- Mirrors

- Pink and red home furnishings

- Plants and flowers—especially with pink or red blossoms

- Candles and lights—especially pink ones

- Personalized ceremonies and rituals

- Red envelopes and "wish" boxes

- Paintings, posters, pictures, figurines and other objects

You'll learn lots of ways to use these as we explore the five phases of the Relationship Cycle. Basic guidelines for working with these and other feng shui objects are also provided on pages 205-212 in the back of the book.

There are as many different ways to activate power spots as there are individuals on this planet, so be sure to look for ways to put your own special spin on the traditional feng shui empowerment and enhancement techniques.

Principle 8:
Work on Yourself as well as Your Home

If you don't take care of yourself—emotionally and physically—it will be harder to fully appreciate the benefits of feng shui. The first Fast Feng Shui book includes an introduction to a variety of ways you can make sure your personal *chi* is as strong, balanced, and positive as possible. These include:

- Aromatherapy

- Flower essences and remedies

- Color therapies of various kinds

- Massage & chiropractic treatment

- Traditional Chinese Medicine

- Ayurveda

- Qigong & Tai Chi Chuan

- Yoga

- Meditation

While we don't focus much on personal *chi* in this book, it's worth asking yourself how much good it will do to empower your love life if you are too stressed, tired, or just plain cranky to make a good impression on the people you meet or to fully enjoy a new relationship.

If you are committed to turning your love life around, be sure to include self-care and renewal as part of your overall plan.

Principle 9:
Evaluate Your Results

No one can predict exactly what results you will see from applying feng shui to your love life. Sometimes the results are quick and dramatic, and other times it can take what feels like forever for the energy to shift. You may receive exactly what you hoped for, or the results may come in a completely unexpected form.

Often the effects of feng shui are not exactly what you had in mind. You may find that you are meeting a lot of new people or going on a lot of dates, but still not connecting with anyone special. You might use feng shui with the intention of moving a stuck relationship "forward," and end up breaking up with that person. Or perhaps you meet someone who looks just like the man or woman of your dreams, but the rush of excitement and passion you expected just isn't there.

None of these mean feng shui isn't working—they mean you may have been overlooking a key insight, or that there are key lessons for you to learn before you can progress in your romantic life. Perhaps what you think you want isn't really what you need. You may have rushed into dating when you most need to spend time releasing past relationships and rediscovering yourself before you are ready to connect with someone new.

When feng shui seems to trigger the end of a relationship, it's often because someone even better is on the verge of appearing in your life. If your "dream" partner turns out to be a dud, be open to meeting someone who isn't quite so perfect on the surface, but who has all the inner qualities you are looking for.

Feng shui works best when you remain open to a variety of outcomes. Trust that if you have an open heart and a welcoming attitude, the universe will bring you exactly what you need to move you forward on your path. Feng shui is a terrific tool for getting your love life back on track, but you still may have to go around the Relationship Cycle a time or two before you meet your perfect match. Remind yourself to see each setback as a valuable learning experience, and remember that true love is worth waiting for!

Feng shui teaches us the importance of living in alignment with universal energy. As you achieve greater serenity and clarity in your home environment by removing the distractions caused by clutter and disorganization, blocked or harmful *chi*, and all the little things that don't support or assist you, you will be better able to live in each moment as your authentic self.

Only by radiating your true self in thought, word, and deed, will you attract the partner who best matches and complements your own natural magnificence. Feng shui creates an environment in which you can rediscover and reconnect with yourself—so you can then connect with your perfect partner. This is one reason why the Fast Feng Shui Relationship Cycle begins with the Centering phase.

The Fast Feng Shui Relationship Cycle

The Five Phases of a Romantic Relationship

The Fast Feng Shui approach to transforming your love life is based on the insight that attracting a new partner is only one aspect of what transforming your love life is all about.

For example, if a serious relationship has recently ended, you may benefit most from a period of healing and self-reflection before starting to date again—no matter how eager you may be to connect with your next partner. Or perhaps you've been dating one person exclusively for a while, and are wondering whether or not to make a commitment. This book shows you how to use feng shui to help you progress appropriately and effectively through each stage of the five-phase Relationship Cycle:

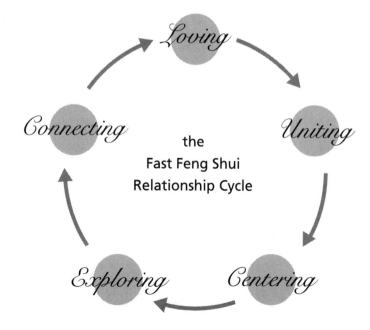

Loving

Connecting

Uniting

the
Fast Feng Shui
Relationship Cycle

Exploring

Centering

The Fast Feng Shui Relationship Cycle is based on the Creative cycle of the five elements*. Each stage of the cycle is associated with one element whose qualities, characteristics, and energy most closely match your situation and goals. By working with the appropriate element at each stage, you can make faster and smoother progress through the Cycle.

PHASE 1: CENTERING

The Relationship Cycle begins with Centering, which is associated with the contracting, inward-focused energy of the METAL element. In this stage you are not in a relationship, and are not actively dating. This may be because you are just now reaching the age when you are ready for a serious adult relationship or because a past relationship has ended and you are starting the cycle again.

Centering is a time for rediscovering your sense of self and for creating a strong foundation for being an equal partner in your next relationship. In the Centering chapter, we'll explore how feng shui can help you release past loves, heal a lonely heart, and prepare for a new romance.

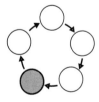

PHASE 2: EXPLORING

The Exploring stage of the Relationship Cycle is associated with the flowing quality of the WATER element. The inward focus of the Centering phase

---

* If you are not familiar with the five feng shui elements and how they interact—or if you could use a quick refresher—take a few minutes to review pages 198-201 in the back of the book before continuing with this section.

turns outward, and you feel ready to get involved in a relationship again. You start dating actively, and are open to new people and experiences, but there is not yet one special person in your life.

Phase 2 focuses on expanding your social life and helping you meet a wide range of new people. If the idea of getting back on the dating scene makes you cringe, the Exploring chapter will help you "get your feet wet" again more comfortably.

PHASE 3: CONNECTING

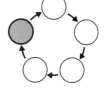

The Connecting phase of the Relationship Cycle is associated with the new beginnings and upward growth of the WOOD element.

In this stage, your focus shifts from meeting new people to exploring possibilities with one particular individual. In the Connecting chapter you'll learn to support a budding relationship by using feng shui to create a home environment that encourages romance.

PHASE 4: LOVING

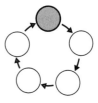

The Loving phase of the Relationship Cycle is associated with the energizing, passionate qualities of the FIRE element. This is the head-over-heels, mad-about-you experience of mutual infatuation that is so much fun and what we are thinking of when we yearn to be "in love."

In this stage you and your special someone are practically inseparable, and are recognized by friends and family as a couple.

In the Loving chapter we'll look at how feng shui can help you enhance the longevity of this often short-lived phase by identifying and correcting barriers to communication and intimacy.

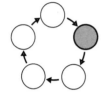

PHASE 5: UNITING

The Uniting stage of a relationship is associated with the stable and nurturing qualities of the EARTH element. Here you and your love are ready to make a commitment and build a life together, and you either become engaged or decide to live together.

In the Uniting chapter, we'll take a quick look at how feng shui can support a stable and long-lasting partnership filled with peace, joy, and love.

By tailoring your feng shui activities to the special focus and needs of each stage of the Relationship Cycle, your progress through the five phases will be smoother and more successful. And when a relationship ends, you'll know how to start the cycle again with ease, grace, and confidence.

JOURNALING

Obviously, not all relationships make it through all phases of the cycle—if they did, we'd still be paired up with our high school sweethearts. The rate at which you move through each stage can vary tremendously, too. Sometimes you can go from Connecting to Loving in a matter of hours, and there will always be a lucky few who connect with someone while they're still in the Centering phase, and skip over the Exploring stage completely.

What usually occurs, when things happen that fast, is that you end up backtracking at some point and doing the work of earlier stages that may have been rushed through or skipped over in the beginning.

We'll explore each of the five phases in detail throughout the next five chapters. For now, take a few minutes to think about your romantic life—as it is now, and as it has been over the past several years—in terms of this Relationship Cycle:

- What phase of the cycle are you in right now?

- What do you like and not like about that phase?

- Is there a particular stage at which most of your relationships have ended? Why do you think that is?

- What stage feels safest and most comfortable for you? Why?

- What stage is the most difficult for you? Why?

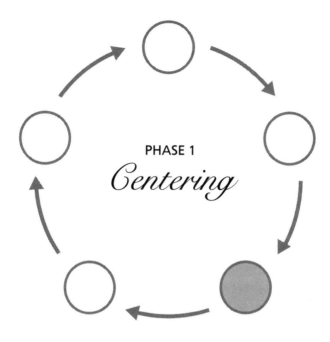

PHASE 1

Centering

The Relationship Cycle begins with the Centering phase. In this stage you are on your own without a romantic partner. You may have been alone for some time, or may have only recently become single again.

Because this phase follows the end of your previous relationship, it is often a time of heartache and sadness. You may be grieving the death of a spouse or partner, feeling knocked off-balance after the stress and anxieties of divorce, or reeling from the pain of an unexpected breakup. On the other hand, you might be experiencing the more positive side of this phase, when the decision to leave an outgrown or limiting relationship brings a welcome feeling of freedom and possibility.

Typically in this stage you are not actively dating. Sometimes that's because you just aren't meeting anyone you feel like going out with (we'll tackle that problem in Phase 2). Or perhaps you are still "licking your wounds" after a difficult breakup, and just aren't ready to face the world of relationships again. Others will celebrate a new-found freedom and independence, and may choose to be on their own for a while. Depending on your circumstances, you may be feeling numb, vulnerable, overwhelmed, relieved, exhilarated, or in a state of chaos.

Some of you may have been dating a lot lately, only to realize that your heart's not in it. That's usually a sign that you've jumped into the Exploring stage (Phase 2) too quickly, without doing the grounding work associated with Phase 1. It's important to take some time to regroup and explore who you are when you're on your own, before looking for a connection with someone new.

Whatever your position and condition may be, look upon the Centering phase as *your* time: a time for recovery when you can release the stress and heartache of a relationship that has ended and create a strong foundation for connecting with someone new.

Your most important tasks in the Centering phase center around emotional healing. They include releasing your attachments to the past and forgiving those who have bruised your heart so you can move forward more easily. This is also a time to rediscover yourself. In this section, you'll learn a variety of feng shui techniques to help you do that.

The Metal Element in Feng Shui

The Centering phase is associated with the METAL element. We can gain a greater understanding of the qualities and objectives of this stage by exploring the meanings and characteristics of metal.

What are some of the qualities that come to mind for you when you think of metal? For some, that might include "cold," "hard," and "sharp," while others may think of metal as "glimmering," "shiny," or "silver and gold."

Pay attention to your gut reaction to METAL and what it may reveal about this phase in your life; is it a positive and rewarding time for you, or a cold and lonely period? There are no right or wrong answers; whatever you are experiencing is appropriate, and an opportunity for insight.

Here are some forms, functions, qualities, and symbolic meanings of metal in daily life:

- *Tools (knives, scissors, axe, etc.)*: cutting away what's not wanted; paring down to the essence; turning things into a usable form

- *Armor*: protection; being ready for anything

- *Scaffolding/framework*: support; something to lean on; holds things up

- *Stapler, paper clips, sewing needle*: holding things together; getting organized; dealing with the details of daily life

- *Keys*: opening new doors; figuring it out

- *Pots and pans*: self-care and nurturing; paying attention to your needs

- *Precious metals, coins*: value; resources; reconnecting with your inner worth

- *Gilt*: glamour; finding ways to pamper yourself; nobility and honor

- *Clean and shiny*: creating a new beginning; incorruptible

- *Strength and durability*: connecting with your inner strength; surviving

- *Work-out weights*: building physical strength; self-development of all kinds

- *Figures/statues*: Ganesh—remover of obstacles; Bodhisattva—enlightenment, serenity, meditation

- *Meditation bells*: be in the moment; pay attention to now, stop dwelling in "if only" and "I wish"

- *Wind chimes*: feng shui cure for protection and activation

- *Mirrors*: (in ancient times, made from polished metal; modern mirrors made with silver backing on glass) self-awareness, perception

- *Alchemy*: turning lead into gold

"Turning lead into gold" is my favorite metaphor for the METAL stage of the Relationship Cycle. You may start out feeling leaden, heavy, sluggish, and maybe even dented, tarnished, and rusty in places. With some help from feng shui and the introspective qualities of METAL, you can emerge shining and triumphant, ready to love and be loved again.

THE FENG SHUI VIEW OF METAL

In feng shui, METAL is associated with the season of autumn, which is a time for harvesting the fruits of one's labors, and with completing one cycle so a new one can begin.

METAL is heavy and cold, and is associated with inward, contracting movement or focus. This can provide a welcome respite from an over-stimulating world, or it may lead to stagnation if it is too strong.

In Traditional Chinese Medicine (TCM), the METAL element is associated with the lungs and large intestine. When we are struggling with the more difficult emotional aspects of the Centering relationship phase—heartache, loss, loneliness—we may feel heaviness in the chest, or experience problems with our digestion.*

When out of balance, the emotional quality of METAL is grief or sadness, and the sound associated with metal is "weeping," which is often a very appropriate reaction to heartache.

The "virtue" or personal quality of METAL *chi* is righteousness. Master Lin Yun, spiritual leader of Black Tibetan Buddhist (BTB) feng shui, teaches that too much METAL energy gives us "porcupine *chi*"—prickly and self-righteous. Too little METAL leads to "choked" *chi*—we become silent, shy, and withdrawn, unable to take appropriate action for ourselves or on the part of others.

JOURNALING

Find a quiet time and place to explore your personal experience of the Centering relationship phase. What insights have you gained from exploring the meanings of METAL energy from a feng shui perspective? Think about what you are experiencing right now, as well as how you may have reacted to the challenges and opportunities of the Centering phase in the past.

---

* I recognize two kinds of metal-stage heartache. When hit with the mild form, you may turn to food for comfort and tend to gain weight. The severe form is what I call "the amazing heartache diet," when you are too miserable, hurt, and confused to eat, and the pounds just melt away.

- How do you usually respond to this phase emotionally?

- How do you respond physically? Do your eating or sleeping patterns and habits change?

- Does your behavior change when you are in the metal phase? Do you withdraw from the world, or throw yourself into action to distract yourself? Do you stop exercising, or become obsessive about working out?

What do you most need to accomplish during your journey through this phase of the relationship cycle? This might be:

- Being able to let go of the past

- A chance to retreat and heal emotionally

- The opportunity to rediscover who you are without the structure of a relationship to define you

- Learning to be comfortable being alone with yourself and/or to nurture yourself

- Reconnecting with your creativity

- Experiencing your home as a place of safety and security

- Connecting with an appropriate counselor, therapist, or support group

Metal Energy and the Ba Gua

The METAL element is associated with two areas of the *ba gua* energy map: *dui gua* (creativity and children) and *chien gua* (helpful friends and travel). These are located on the right side of the *ba gua*, below the relationship area (*kun gua*):

dui
creativity,
children

chien
helpful friends,
travel

If you are placing the *ba gua* according to the compass directions, *dui gua* (creativity and children) is in the west, and *chien gua* (helpful friends and travel), is northwest.

The standard definitions of the different areas of the *ba gua* cover a wide range of qualities and associations. For example, you've learned to think of *dui gua* as the "children and creativity" area. From the perspective of the challenges and tasks of Centering, *dui gua* supports the creative work of redefining yourself as a single person and discovering what that means for you. Artists and non-artists alike may turn to various forms of creative expression to assist in self-discovery and in healing a bruised heart.

If you have children, you may find that working on this area will help you adapt more easily to your new family structure. Or perhaps Centering will provide you with a welcome opportunity to reconnect with your inner child and learn to be playful again.

Activating *chien gua* (helpful friends and travel) can be very beneficial if you need the assistance of a therapist, counselor, or support group to help you with your transition or with other relationship issues. Need a faster fix? You can work with *chien gua* as you plan that much-needed spa vacation or arrange a trip to visit a friend who lives far away.

Because *dui* (creativity/children) and *chien* (helpful friends/ travel) *guas* are associated with METAL, EARTH-type cures and colors are appropriate here.* Avoid placing too much WATER energy in either of these *guas*, as it will deplete the METAL, and remember that FIRE will melt METAL unless you also add EARTH to create a three-element arc of the Creative cycle.

Take a moment now to think about what *dui* and *chien guas* might mean for you as you move through the Centering phase. Do you have specific needs or issues that could benefit from using feng shui in these areas?

We can explore all the other *guas* as well, to see how they relate to the issues and challenges of the Centering phase.

YOUR CENTERING BA GUA

Draw a nine-square grid in your notebook or on a piece of paper (or photocopy the *ba gua* template on page 204). Write "Centering" in the middle (*tai chi*) square.

For *dui* (creativity and children) and *chien* (helpful friends and travel) *guas*—the middle and bottom of the right side—write in any special meaning these areas have for you at this time, based on your personal issues and goals for the Centering phase.

---

* You can find information about the cycles of the elements and feng shui objects in the Appendix. If you are new to feng shui, you may want to consult the first Fast Feng Shui book or other books for beginners to learn more about working with the *ba gua*, and how to use feng shui cures.

Now think about the other *guas*. If you can't remember what goes where, refer to the *ba gua* map on page 188. (You may want to stick a paper clip or sticky note on that page so you can find it again easily.) Think about any personal meaning the other *guas* may have for you in the Centering stage, and note them in the appropriate place. There are no right or wrong answers; this is your personal *ba gua*, and it's okay to leave some spaces blank.

Here's an example of a Centering *ba gua*:

things I am grateful for	how I want others to perceive me	self-nurturing
be a strong family unit	CENTERING	take an art class
reconnect with my spiritual side	clarify my life path	find a support group

The final step in this exercise is to look at your personal *ba gua* definitions and choose which *guas* are your top priorities for the Centering stage. For example, if your strongest need is for nurturing, then *kun gua* (relationships) is your priority area. Or perhaps your sense of identity has been shaken up by the end of a long relationship, in which case *li gua* (reputation) and *ken gua* (self-understanding) will be important. Your change in circumstances may have triggered a related shift in your relationship with your parents or siblings, making *jen gua* (family) important for you now.

Find Your Centering Power Spots

Remember how you looked for overlaps when locating your relationship power spots? If you skipped that section, or you need to refresh your memory of how to use the *ba gua*, this would be a good time to review pages 24-26; we're going to use the same method to find your Centering power spots.

Get out the floor plans on which you marked your relationship power spots. Now find the *gua*(s) you picked for your Centering focus on the floor plans for your home, bedroom, and other key rooms. Look to see if any of your relationship power spots overlap with them.

For example, let's say you picked *chien gua* (helpful friends) as a priority area for this phase. Where is *chien gua* in the room that is in *kun gua* (relationships) in your house?

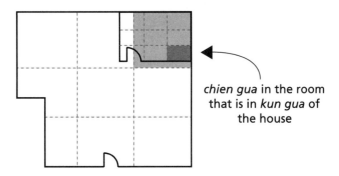

chien gua in the room that is in *kun gua* of the house

Now find the room that is in the helpful friends area (*chien gua*)of your house. Where is *kun gua* within that room?

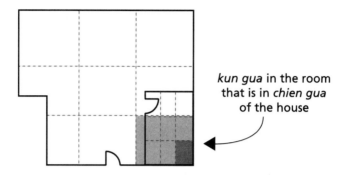

kun gua in the room
that is in *chien gua*
of the house

You may find several overlap areas, or none. If you don't find any areas of overlap, use your strongest relationship power spot or your target *gua* in your bedroom as your Centering power spot.

WORKING WITH YOUR CENTERING POWER SPOTS

Now that you've found your Centering power spots, you can:

- Make sure they are clean, tidy, and free of clutter

- Adjust the lighting as needed (bright lights activate a space and assist mental clarity and problem-solving; softer lighting is good for relaxation and meditation)

- Activate the space with a traditional or personal feng shui cure. For example, you could hang a wind chime in a *chien gua* (helpful friends) power spot, and empower it to help you connect with a good support group or therapist.

- Add appropriate imagery (artwork, photographs, figurines). For example, you could place photos of yourself and your children (and their grandparents or other relatives, as appropriate) in a *jen gua* (family) power spot and empower them to help you build or sustain strong family ties.

You can find basic guidelines for using feng shui cures and activations on pages 205-212 in the back of the book. Remember to use your body-speech-mind empowerments (see pages 10-12) with any changes and enhancements that you make.

ACTION STEPS

The rest of this chapter details specific things you can do to assist you in moving gracefully and successfully through the Centering phase of the Relationship Cycle. They include:

- **Mundane cures**: physical changes you can make to your home to make it a supportive and empowering environment for transition and growth

- **Transcendental cures**: rituals for removing negative *chi* and shifting your own energy

- **Insight work**: meditations and journaling exercises to help you reconnect with yourself and your environment

Every home is different, and you each have a unique situation, needs, and goals. One person may benefit most from beginning a daily meditation practice and focusing on internal work for a while before tackling household changes. Someone else may feel a strong urge to rearrange furniture and clear stuff out, to create a shift in physical surroundings before settling down to focus, breathe, and relax. Pay attention to what your body is telling you—does it want to curl up and retreat or jump into action?

Remember that the "KISS" principle (*Keep it simple, Sweetie!*) is just as true for feng shui as it is in the rest of your life. Don't try to make every possible adjustment at once. Read through the suggestions in this chapter with a pad of sticky notes at hand. Get out your notebook, and make a list of at least three things you want to start with. Plan to complete them within three days, if possible. Do make an effort to include at least one item from each category (mundane, transcendental, and insight) in your action plan.

Keep in mind that feng shui is about creating balance in your home and your life. If you feel most like curling up in a ball and retreating from the world, make that the core of your immediate plans, but be sure to include a physical activity as well, so you don't become totally sedated. If you're revved up and ready to change your entire house around, be sure to include some meditation and quiet time as well, so you don't burn yourself out.

Listen to your intuition, too; if you have an overwhelming urge to clean out a particular closet, weed the garden, or repaint the kitchen, go ahead and tackle it, even if it isn't included in this chapter or located in one of your power spots. You'll feel so much better when it's done. While you're at it, allow your inner wisdom to suggest reasons you might have been drawn to that particular chore, and explore any symbolic connections or meanings it may have for you. Record your insights in your feng shui journal.

Feng Shui for the Centering Phase

Releasing the Past

One of the most difficult challenges of the Centering phase is to be fully present and aware in the here and now. We can get so caught up in "if only" and "what if" thoughts that it can be difficult to be fully functional in the present.

I don't mean that you should ignore your past, or not spend time reflecting on and learning from your experiences in past relationships. I do mean that our emotional reactions to the end of a relationship—whether it happened last week or years ago—can be so powerful that they interfere with our ability to move forward and live an authentic, self-aware life.

Here's a quick quiz: How much of your time over the past few weeks has been spent living in the past or fantasizing about the future? This includes:

- Thinking about an ex-partner*

- Feeling self-pity because he or she left you

- Feeling guilty because you are the one who left

- Feeling guilty because you didn't get it together to leave sooner

---

* I use this term loosely, to mean any past partner with whom you are no longer romantically involved, whether as the result of divorce, separation, breaking up, or the death of a spouse or partner.

- Feeling guilty because you did something (whether intentionally or not) to trigger the break-up

- Wanting your husband, wife, or lover back

- Getting lost in memories of the good times

- Asking yourself, God, or your ex, "Why?" or "Why me?"

- Having imaginary conversations with your ex, in which you get to say everything that's on your mind

- Feeling angry or resentful about his or her behavior

- Feeling jealous of your ex's new partner, or of happily coupled friends

- Regretting past things you thought, said, or did to or about your ex

- Regretting lost opportunities to say or do something to or with your ex

- Replaying arguments in your head, so you win this time

- Plotting, planning, and scheming to get even or to get him/her back (even if you don't actually plan to *do* any of it)

- Getting angry about something that you expect your ex to do (or not do), when it hasn't even happened yet

- Worrying about the future

- Wondering if you will ever find love again

Did any of these apply to you? Congratulations, you're human! But what do you do when you still live with these thoughts, day after day, even though you would like to let go of them? With feng shui, you can clear your head and your heart by clearing old energy out of your space. Here are some ways you can do that.

TAKE A CLEANSING BATH

If your break-up has been especially rough, and you feel that there is a lot of negative energy clinging to you—anger, resentment, harsh words heard or said, physical threats, self-blame—an orange peel bath can help release that psychic sludge.

The basic procedure is simple: peel an orange, then break the peel into nine pieces and add it to your bath water. As you soak in the tub, visualize the orange-scented water rinsing all negative energy away and protecting you from future negativity.

You can make this special bath even more powerful by:

- Using the dispelling mudra* to empower the bath water to clean and protect you, before climbing into it

- Repeating this bath every night for nine nights

- Creating a personal ritual around the bath. Light a candle or some incense, play soothing music, add flowers to the tub along with the orange peel, say a prayer asking for assistance in releasing unwanted attachments, or whatever feels right for you.

- Using orange essense aromatherapy body lotion after the bath

SWIM IN THE OCEAN

Salt is a powerful cleanser, and is good for removing negativity. If you live near the ocean and your climate and season permit, swim in the salt water as often as possible. Visualize all negative energy washing away, leaving you clean and renewed.

---

* See page 10 for instructions on how to use the dispelling mudra

GET A NEW BED

If you're getting eight full hours of shut-eye a night, you're spending a full third of your life in your bed. Even if you get by with less sleep than you need, that's still a major chunk of your life. While you are sleeping your pillow, sheets, blankets, and mattress are absorbing your energy, and that of whoever is sharing your bed.

When a long-term relationship ends, the person who leaves gets a fresh start and whoever keeps the furniture keeps all that old energy with it. Every night, you're sleeping in energy that holds you in the past. That's why feng shui experts advise getting a new bed following a divorce.

Given the cost of furniture, buying a new bed may not be an option for you right now. Do not try to economize by getting a second-hand bed or mattress! If you think sleeping in your own old energy is yucky, why would you want to sleep in a stranger's energetic nest? If you can afford a new mattress and box spring, this is a great time to get them. And if you feel inspired to get a new bed frame, too, that's even better.

BUY NEW BEDDING

If you can't afford a complete fresh start, do at least spring for (in order of priority):

- new pillows
- new sheets
- a new mattress pad
- new blankets

As you're changing your bed, mattress, or bedding, remember to empower your new furnishings to provide a fresh, comfortable place for you to sleep, completely free of old relationship energy.

CLEAN OUT UNDER YOUR BED

Anything that is stored under your bed is contributing to blocked or stuck energy in your bedroom, and may be affecting you on a subconscious level while you sleep.

If you have boxes of old stuff stashed under the bed, go through them to make sure there are no relics from past relationships lurking there. You especially want to remove any objects or clothes that belong to an ex-partner, and things that they gave you to which you may have a strong emotional attachment, and all photographs of past loves.

Ideally, you will keep the space under your bed completely open, so fresh *chi* can circulate around your bed and help activate your love life. If you must use the space under your bed for storage, it's best to only keep bed-related items—such as extra sheets, blankets, or pillows—there. Avoid storing anything under the bed that could disturb your sleep. This includes items associated with movement or mental effort, such as shoes, exercise equipment or workout clothes, books or papers, and so on.

Be especially careful not to keep any metal objects under the bed, as METAL energy is associated with sharp or cutting *chi*, and you don't want to feel under attack while you sleep.

MOVE INTO A DIFFERENT BEDROOM

You may have no choice about which room to sleep in, but if you do, consider relocating, at least for a while. Sleeping in a different space will help you make the transition away from old energy and attachments. Check your floor plan to see what *guas* any available spaces are in, and see if any of them are in your relationship or Centering power spots. Avoid a bedroom over the garage, as your energy and sleep could be affected by the disruptive energy associated by cars pulling in and out.

Do choose a space that is quiet and private, so you can get the rest you need. Usually the back areas of the house are the best bedroom locations.

If you do switch rooms, use this opportunity to decorate or accessorize with some favorite personal things. Otherwise, you may feel like you're camping out in the guest room. Make the room yours in whatever ways feel appropriate to you.

As you read through this book, you'll find lots of suggestions for using feng shui in the bedroom, so don't rush out and buy too many new things until you've had a chance to make your feng shui shopping list.

CLEAR THE AIR WITH SOUND VIBRATIONS

Sound vibrations help to loosen stale, stuck energy. You can use a rattle, bells, a wind chime, even bang on a metal cook pot, to shake things up. Walk through your entire house or focus on one problem area where stuff and clutter has piled up—a sure sign of stuck energy in that area.

If there are certain areas of your home that used to be your ex's space—anything from a dresser drawer or one section of a bookcase to a separate room in your house—make some noise there to shake up that old energy and reclaim the space for yourself.

If clearing and cleaning your space seems like a bigger chore than you're up for right now, ring a bell all around your body and let the sound waves energize you.

CLEAN YOUR CARPETS

Rugs and carpets collect old energy along with dirt, dust, crumbs, and pet hair. Make sure to include a thorough carpet cleaning along with your other energy-clearing methods, especially if you have been using the sound cure to loosen stale or stuck *chi*.

SMUDGE YOUR SPACE

The smoke from smoldering sage leaves is a powerful energetic cleanser. You can buy dried sage "smudge sticks" at most New Age stores. Light the end, then gently blow out the flame to leave the embers still glowing and smoking. Hold the smudge stick over an ashtray and carry it through the space you are clearing. You can smudge yourself, too, while you are at it: pass the smoke up and down the front and back of your body, and make sure to get the top of your head, too.

GIVE YOUR HOME AN ORANGE-PEEL BATH

This orange peel cure removes stale or negative *chi* from your home. Buy fresh oranges for this cure, rather than any that you already have in the house.

1. Peel three fresh oranges, and tear each peel into nine pieces (for a total of 27 pieces). Place the pieces in a large bowl and add about a cup of bottled or filtered water.

2. Standing in the center of each room, dip your fingers in the orange-scented water and flick some of it in all directions using the dispelling mudra (see page 10). At the same time, visualize negative *chi* being dispersed and repeat the mantra *om mani padme hum* nine times.

3. Take a piece of orange peel and break off little bits, scattering them all around the sides of the room, and repeat in each room of the house. If there is orange peel and water left over, place the bowl in the center of the house over night.

4. Leave the orange peel for 24 hours. It will absorb negative *chi*, which you can then easily remove from your space as you sweep or vacuum up the bits of orange peel and throw them away.

PERFORM A SPACE CLEARING CEREMONY

A formal space clearing ceremony is the most powerful way to remove stale and negative energy from your space. You can do a space clearing on your own or with a friend or family member.

This is the method I use to clear my own home. It is based on the techniques taught by Karen Kingston and Denise Linn, and will give you a good idea of the steps and materials involved. If you wish to do a serious space clearing of your home, I highly recommend that you get a copy of Karen's book, *Creating Sacred Space with Feng Shui*, or Denise's *Space Clearing* (see the Resources section of the Appendix for details) and learn from the experts.

The day of the full or new moon is a good time for a space clearing, or choose any other day that is auspicious for you, when you will not be distracted, interrupted, or feeling rushed. Ladies, do not perform a space clearing while you have your period.

Your house should be clean and tidy before you begin. If you have a monster clutter problem, a space clearing can loosen up all the old energy that is clogging up your home. This will make it easier to get started with your clutter clearing efforts. Getting rid of your clutter will shake a lot more energy loose, so you'll probably want to do another space clearing when you are done.

Preparation

Take a bath or shower, then dry off and dress in loose, comfortable clothing, preferably white. If your house is very private, and you are comfortable naked, you could do this in the nude. Do not use any fragrance (including scented body lotions), cosmetics, or hair styling products. Do not wear a watch or any metal jewelry or hair clips. If you can get by without your eyeglasses, leave them off, too. Go barefoot.

Set up or clear a small table in the center of the home or in the living room. Cover the table with a beautiful piece of fabric or a clean tablecloth.

Set up a candle, a stick of incense, a bottle of spring water, a bowl or dish, and some fresh flowers ready on the table. You will also need at least one brass bell. If you don't have any bells, a wind chime can be used instead. If you have a drum or loud rattle you can use those, too. Set out your bells and other instruments on the table.

Put the dogs out (cats, too), if you have pets and a yard.

Open at least one window. If it's cold out, an inch will do.

I like to listen to soothing music as I get ready, so I feel calm and relaxed when I perform the procedure. Be sure to turn music off when it's time to begin.

Invocation

Stand in the center of your space, and take a few slow, deep breaths. Mentally extend your consciousness throughout the entire house. State your intention to purify the space (aloud or to yourself), and visualize how radiant and full of *chi* your home will be when you are done.

Light the candle and incense. Pour the bottled water into the bowl, and float the flower blossoms in the water.

Ask for assistance from whatever guides, spirits, angels, saints, or deities are appropriate to your spiritual practice. Call on the guardian spirits of the house and of the earth, air, water, and sky to help you.

Using the dispelling mudra (page 10), flick some of the water to each of the four directions: east, south, west, and north.

Clear the Space

Starting at the main entrance, go all around the inside perimeter of the space, feeling for areas of stuck energy. Hold your palms a few inches from the wall as you walk around the room, and try to feel any variations in the energy. There may be places where the energy feels sticky or heavy, or where you feel a prickly or tingling sensation in your hands. You may not be able to feel the energy without practice, so if you don't notice anything at all that's okay. Odd or unpleasant smells and unusual warm or cold spots in the house also can indicate areas where the energy may need to be cleared.

Starting again at the front door, move around the sides of each room and clap your hands, bang your drum, or shake a rattle to loosen the energy. Pay special attention to corners and to any areas where you sensed stuck energy during your first circuit of the house.

When you are done, wash your hands in running water to rinse off any stale energy that may have stuck to them.

Purify the Space

Go around the space once more, using your bell or wind chime this time, ringing it continually so the sound never fades. If you have several bells to use, start with the one with the lowest tone, then do a circuit with a middle tone, and finish with a circuit with the highest tone.

Listen for any shifts in the tone of each bell. If you come to a place where the sound seems dull, ring in that spot until the tone improves.

If you are able to sense energy well with your hands, it's a good idea to go around the space once more, checking for any spots where the energy is still stuck or sticky. Clap loudly in those spots a few times, then purify that area with the bells again.

Bless the Space

Wash your hands under running water again, then stand in the center of your space and visualize the entire home glowing with a bright, pure light that extends into every corner and fills the home with peace and love.

Thank your guardian or assisting spirits for their help, and say a prayer to close the ceremony. You may wish to spend a few minutes sitting quietly to absorb and appreciate the clean, fresh energy of your home.

As you can see, a thorough space clearing is a bit of a production, especially if you live in a large house or have a significant amount of housework to do first. I assure you that it is well worth the effort. Your home will shine, and your spirits are sure to feel lifted and renewed.

If you lack confidence in your own abilities to do a good space-clearing, you may want to hire a trained practitioner to work with you. Karen Kingston and Denise Linn both offer professional space clearing training programs. Check the Resources pages for contact information, or visit **www.fastfengshui.com** for links to their web sites.

HO'OPONO'OPONO

Ho'opono'opono is a Hawaiian ritual for releasing emotional and energetics ties to negative or difficult experiences. It can be used to restore balance and harmony to the body and spirit after a trauma, accident, or any situation that leaves you feeling rattled and shaken—even to resolve negative energy lingering from past life experiences. It is often used to heal the damage caused by disagreements within an *ohana* (family group) or among friends.

Because ho'opono'opono relieves the intense negative emotions such as anger, hatred, resentment, grief, guilt, and depression that can follow a difficult break-up, it can be very helpful to you during the Centering phase of the Relationship Cycle.

The instructions I give here are based on the traditional *huna* practice and incorporate some feng shui touches. I have also adapted it to focus specifically on releasing the negative emotions lingering from past romantic attachments. If you have a difficult or dysfunctional family history, you may want to repeat this ritual to forgive and release negative feelings about family members and situations.

You will need one or more pieces of paper, a pen, matches, a stick of incense, and an ashtray or fireplace in which to burn the paper. Begin with a few minutes of quiet meditation to calm and center your mind.

Focus on your intention to release all unwanted emotional and energetic connections to every person for whom you have had romantic feelings, wishes, or intentions—especially those whom you feel have harmed you physically or emotionally. Include anyone toward whom you have felt ill will about a romantic situation. This might include a friend or family member who did not approve of or support you in a particular relationship or situation.

Review in your mind all the people involved in all of these circumstances. Get out your paper and pen, and make a list of these individuals, noting also the relevant situations and any specific behaviors or actions involved. Your complete list may be lengthy; that's okay. Think of how good it will feel to clear out all that old negativity, anger, blame, hurt, and resentment.

The traditional ritual includes an invocation to all family, relatives, and ancestors to assist in the cleansing. If you have a difficult relationship with anyone in your family, focus on asking for the assistance of that person's highest spirit. You may also wish to ask for assistance from a particular guide, saint, or deity from your spiritual practice.

Light your incense, and visualize the smoke communicating your pure intentions to all people, spirits, or powers involved. Read the following request aloud (or memorize and recite it):

> *I call on all the poe amaukua (highest selves) to work together and hear my request.*
>
> *I, [state your name], and my highest self and ancestors wish to do a Ho'opono'opono for myself and my family and all of the people who have affected my experience of love and romance.*
>
> *Cleanse, purify, release, and sever all negative and harmful memories and all unwanted feelings and impulses that have been created or experienced from the beginning to the present, and transmute these into pure light... and it is done.*

Now burn the papers on which you wrote your list, making sure they are completely reduced to ash. As the paper is burning, use the dispelling mudra (page 10), repeat the mantra *om mani padme hum* nine times and visualize that all of the negative connections have been completely cleared away.

SHUT UP ALREADY!

Reverend Mary Omwake of Unity Church of Maui reminds us that "forgiving someone means you don't tell that story any more." If you have been bitching and moaning about someone or something, try *not* talking about it for a week and see what a difference that makes to your energy.

Once you've decided to let go of a grudge, talking about it doesn't feel good any more because those negative words hold you in the past. Be mindful of the stories you tell, and how you choose to express yourself about your life.

DEEP-CLEAN YOUR BEDROOM

It may be unrealistic to attempt a thorough cleaning of your entire home all at once—if tackling everything is an overwhelming task, narrow your focus to your bedroom. Set aside a weekend day to do this. If you have a clutter problem, take care of that first. Instead of trying to clear all the clutter from all your relationship power spots at once, make your bedroom your top priority.

If you are a neatnik, you'll probably love the idea of really getting the place clean. If you hate housework, remind yourself that this is the beginning of the transformation of your love life. Plan a reward for when you are done, such as a massage or beauty treatment. I don't recommend "shopping therapy" now—you want to be clearing out your space, not bringing more future clutter in.

- Ceiling: remove dust and cobwebs from ceiling moldings and corners; wash/dust light fixtures and replace any dead bulbs

- Walls: dust tops of window frames; dust frames of pictures and wash the glass

- Wash windows

- Wash or dust doors

- Furniture: wash, dust, polish as needed; wash/vacuum slipcovers and upholstery, especially under couch cushions

- Stuff: wash or dust objects; return anything out of place to where it belongs

- Put all clothes and laundry away

- Clean out your dresser, closet and armoire

- Vacuum, sweep, wash floors

WINNOW YOUR PHOTOGRAPHS

Go through your house and find *all* of your photographs of your ex-partner or partners. I mean all of them! That includes the lovely framed ones in the living room as well as the photo albums on the bookcase, the shoeboxes full of loose prints in the closet, and the snapshot that somehow ended up in the kitchen drawer.

Don't panic, I'm not going to tell you to throw them out. I just want you to go through them and make appropriate choices. Visual images are extremely powerful energetically, so pictures from past relationships—even when they're out of sight or so familiar you don't even notice them anymore—help to hold you in the past.

It is completely appropriate to keep cherished photographs of a husband, wife, or lover who has died, or of the ex-spouse who is a co-parent of your children. However, if you are looking forward to meeting someone new, it's a good idea to move them out of your bedroom and living room (where you will see them frequently), and from any of your relationship power spots. *Jen gua* (family) is a good place to keep family photographs of all kinds. If your kids want to have pictures of their other parent around, you can suggest that their room would be a good place.

If you want to banish all traces of a certain someone, tearing those pictures up and burning the pieces and then flushing the ashes down the toilet can be very therapeutic, if that's the kind of closure you need. If you do this, have fun with it. Invite some friends over to help, or make a private ceremony out of it. Use the body-speech-mind empowerment, and congratulate yourself on letting go!

Often you'll find lots of pictures of family holidays, vacations, or group events you'd like to hold on to, and there's Mr. or Ms. turned-out-to-be-Wrong right in the middle of the gathering. These are best kept in a photo album or other storage where you won't see them unless you look for them. Again, be sure to choose a storage space that isn't in one of your relationship power spots.

Feng Shui to Lift Your Spirits

The Centering phase of the Relationship Cycle can turn out to be tremendously liberating and empowering. But that doesn't mean it's always a lot of fun. Depression (along with loneliness, anger, resentment, and heartache) is one of the most common emotions people have to deal with in this phase.

When you are feeling down and dreary, it can be difficult to approach feng shui with the necessary enthusiasm and hopeful anticipation of better things to come. If you are depressed, here are some feng shui and related things you can do to lift your spirits.

ENERGIZE YOUR BED

Get a solid red fitted sheet, and place it over your box spring or mattress. It doesn't have to be visible: you can put it underneath your regular sheets or mattress pad if you like. Using the body-speech-mind method described on pages 10-12, empower this red sheet to lift your *chi* while you sleep. Visualize waking up every morning feeling more cheerful, energized, and optimistic.

ACTIVATE THE TAI CHI

Any changes that you make to the center of your home (the *tai chi*) will affect the entire home. Hanging a large faceted crystal ball in the *tai chi* is a good way to lift the energy of your space.

BRING MORE NATURE CHI INTO THE HOUSE

Live green plants are a good way to bring positive energy into the home. Stop by a local nursery (the garden kind, not the kindergarten type!) and pick up three lush green potted plants. Place one where it will be the first thing you see when you enter your home.

Place another where it is the first thing you see when you enter your living room, and place the third one in your bedroom.

CHEER UP YOUR CHI WITH FRESH FLOWERS

Fresh, fragrant flowers are a wonderful way to uplift drooping spirits and sagging *chi*. If there has been a lot of sadness in your home lately—or you need a change of luck—try this method for bringing joy and good fortune back into the home:

Day 1: Place a bouquet of fresh, fragrant flowers in a vase in a power spot in your living room. Empower the flowers to lift the *chi* of your home, and leave them in place for three days. Change the water daily, so it stays fresh.

Day 4: Place a bouquet of a *different* variety of fresh, fragrant flowers in a vase in a power spot in your bedroom. Empower it to lift the *chi*, and leave it in place for three days, changing the water daily. (The first batch of flowers can remain in place; check them daily and remove any that begin to wilt.)

Day 7: Place a bouquet of a third variety of fresh, fragrant flowers in a vase in a power spot in your kitchen. Empower it, and leave it for three days, changing the water daily. (If any of the flowers in the living room and bedroom are still fresh, they can remain in place; check them daily and remove any that begin to wilt.)

Repeat this cycle twice more, for a total of nine bouquets of fragrant flowers over a period of 27 days. It is essential to use *fragrant* flowers. Although you should not use the same variety of flowers twice in a row, you can repeat varieties over the 27 days.

Take a few moments at least once a day throughout the 27 days to hold your focus, visualize the desired change, and repeat your affirmation.

OPEN THE WINDOWS

If the air in your house is stale, the energy will be, too, and it will be harder for you to feel good about anything. A simple breath of fresh air for your house can help shift the *chi* and your spirits.

A quick way to get a change of *chi* into your home is to open all your windows and doors and leave them open for at least 15 minutes. The best time to do this is between 11 PM and 1 AM, when the *chi* of the day is shifting; you can use that energetic shift to change the *chi* in your house. You don't have to open every window all the way; an inch or two will do. If you can do this when the air is clear and fresh-smelling and there is a gentle breeze, that's even better.

BALANCE YOUR EATING HABITS

If you are eating too much, or don't feel like eating anything at all, your energy and health will suffer along with your mood. A faceted crystal ball over your dining table will balance the *chi* of the dining area. Empower it to help you achieve better eating habits.

For this cure to work, you need to eat a real meal at the table at least once a day, instead of scarfing down a pint of ice cream on the couch, retreating to your bedroom with a pile of brownies, or heading to the gym to work out instead of eating.

Use placemats or a tablecloth, cloth napkins, and your good dishes and flatware. Put a vase of flowers on the table, play your favorite music, and light some candles. You'd go to all this effort for someone else you cared about, right? Well, you deserve a relaxing, nurturing dinner atmosphere, too.

THE HEART-CALMING MANTRA

This short prayer is wonderful to use when you are feeling stressed or over-stimulated and need to settle down. It helps you shift into a quiet, calm state of mind so you can relax and/or focus on the task at hand, and is a good way to begin any meditation practice or ritual (such as the Ho'opono'opono method on pages 68-70). It goes like this:

gate gate	(gah-tay gah-tay)
para gate	(pah-rah gah-tay)
para sam gate	(pah-rah sam gah-tay)
bodhi swaha	(boh-dee sva-ha)

Repeat the mantra nine times. You probably think it's a no-brainer to count to nine, but it's amazingly easy to lose count once you get going. If you use the heart-calming mudra (below) you can use your fingers to keep track.

If you are not comfortable chanting in Sanskrit, you can substitute any brief prayer that helps you center yourself and calm your heart and mind.

THE HEART-CALMING MUDRA

As you say the heart-calming mantra, hold your hands in the heart-calming mudra: palms up, left hand on top of right hand, with tips of thumbs touching. Rest the backs of your hands on your lap, or hold the mudra at heart-level.

To keep track of your nine mantras, gently press one finger of your right hand against your left hand with each repetition of the mantra. Start with your pinky and work up to the thumb and back down again.

Count your thumb only once, so it goes like this: (1) pinky, (2) ring finger, (3) middle finger, (4) index finger, (5) thumb, (6) index, (7) middle, (8) ring, (9) pinky.

You can use this mudra on its own any time, with or without the mantra and may hold it as long as you like. (I use it a lot on airplanes and whenever I feel nervous or tense.)

A CALMING MEDITATION

This simple breathing technique is one of my favorite ways to relax and clear my heart and mind of tension. If you've read the first Fast Feng Shui book, you will have already learned this technique. I chose to include it again here because it is such an effective way to ease heartache and depression. Like the heart-calming mantra, it is a good way to begin any meditative practice or ritual (you may want to use them both), or can be done any time on its own.

If you are feeling particularly stressed or miserable, do this first thing every morning and at night before bed every day for nine, 27, or 108 consecutive days.

Sit with your back straight in an upright chair, or cross-legged on the floor with a cushion under your hips, with your hands in the heart-calming mudra. Close your eyes, relax, and take a few deep breaths. Repeat the heart-calming mantra nine times.

1. Take a long, slow, deep breath, inhaling through the mouth, and imagine that your entire body is filling with bright white light. The light fills every cell in your body, and absorbs all illness, tension, fatigue, and negativity.

2. Exhale in eight short puffs followed by a ninth long puff that extends until your lungs are completely empty. As you exhale, imagine a cloud of dark grey negativity leaving your body and dissolving into nothing.

3. Repeat this inhale-exhale pattern eight times, for a total of nine breaths. I like to visualize the grey exhale becoming lighter with each breath, so by the ninth breath the exhale is clear and clean, and my body is completely free of negativity.

4. Sit quietly for a few moments after you are done, and notice any shifts in your mood and energy.

FOCUS ON THE POSITIVE

I know first-hand how annoying it is to be told to look at the bright side when, so far as you're concerned, all sides are looking pretty grim right now. Nevertheless, I suggest that you do this:

Get out your feng shui journal, turn to a fresh page, and draw an empty *ba gua* grid. Or, make yet another copy of the *ba gua* grid on page 204.

For each *gua*, come up with at least three things that you are grateful for. These can be little things, or great big ones. What they are doesn't matter, so long as you come up with three. When you are done, go over your completed gratitude map, and look at how full and blessed your life is! Take this map out and read it—and add to it—every day for at least nine days.

MOVE YOUR BODY

Depression may be the most powerful energy-sapper around, but the best way to beat it is just to get up and get moving. In the first Fast Feng Shui book, I recommend yoga, tai chi chuan, and qigong to balance and restore your energy. You can find links to a variety of web sites about these practices at www.fastfengshui.com. If you can't muster up enthusiasm for trying something new right now, at least lace up your sneakers and go for a walk outdoors. Mom was right when she said that the fresh air would do you good.

GET OUTSIDE

One of the best things you can do for yourself while you are in the Centering phase is to connect with nature and benefit from its healing energy. Connecting with nature can be deeply restorative, and it will assist you in connecting with yourself.

One good way to do this is to spend at least 15 minutes walking outdoors every day, in as natural a setting as possible. Do this every day for 9 or 27 days. Remember to breathe deeply, so you get lots of fresh air into your lungs, and try to keep your attention in the present moment, not somewhere in "what if" or "if only" land.

Below and on the following pages is a meditative practice that I find particularly rejuvenating when my spirits are low or I'm feeling stressed. Depending on where you live, and your local climate and season, there are various ways you can adapt this. I've included a garden version and a beach version here, but you could use this in the woods, a mountain meadow, or beside a stream or river. You can also do this as a visualization at home, or sitting on a park bench during your lunch break.

Garden Meditation

Your back yard may seem to be the perfect spot for this, but if you spend a lot of time there, try a different location for a change of *chi* and scenery. On the other hand, if you've been so overwhelmed or busy lately that you haven't spent time in your own garden, take this opportunity to connect with the natural energy there.

Lie on your back on the ground or in the grass for a few minutes and completely relax. Soft, lush green grass is ideal for this, and if you can be in a garden or park with flowering plants or blossoming trees nearby, that's even better. Completely release your weight into the earth. Allow Mother Earth to support you. Empty your mind, and breathe deeply. Feel the freshness of the air filling your lungs, and allow this clear energy to cleanse you internally.

When you are ready, sit on the ground with your knees up and hands by your side, so the base of your spine, the palms of your hands, and the soles of your feet (bare, if possible) are all touching the earth. Breathe and relax. Quiet your mind. Be completely present in the moment. Just sit for at least five minutes and allow the energy of the earth to recharge and rebalance you.

While you are sitting, feel the grass beneath your hands and feet. Is it cool to the touch, or warm from the sun? Is it soft or tickly? Is the ground dry and hard, or soft from recent rains? Feel your connection to Mother Earth. Release your stress, anxiety, pain, and anger into the earth through your hands and feet, and allow the healing and balancing energy of the earth flow through you.

Close your eyes. What else do you feel? The warmth of the sun? A cool breeze? A muscle ache? Loose hair brushing against your face? The weight of your clothing against your skin?

Listen. What do you hear? Traffic, children, conversations, birds, leaves rustling, a plane passing overhead? Do you hear your own breathing? Allow your awareness to extend further and further outward, and feel your presence and attention connect you to everything in the space around you.

Still with your eyes closed, allow your sense of smell to come into play. What aromas surround you? Do you smell flowers, yourself, a perfume, a hotdog vendor? (If you notice a bad smell, feel free to relocate to another patch of grass that is free of doggie doo or farther from that garbage bin you didn't notice when you first sat down. Take a moment to reground before continuing.)

What do you taste? Breakfast? Lunch? A recent breath mint? Just plain mouth taste?

Slowly open your eyes. What do you see? Take a moment just to absorb whatever is in your field of vision. Does anything look different to you now than it did before you closed your eyes? Do you feel a stronger connection now to the environment around you?

Lie back again, and look up at the sky. Feel the expansive heavens above you and the hugeness of the earth beneath you. Feel how you inhabit the boundary between heaven and earth. Stay with this as long as is comfortable, then slowly sit up. You may want to follow this with some gentle qigong or stretching exercises, or a walking meditation.

Beach Meditation

NOTE: An indoor swimming pool at your health club or community center is really not a good substitute for the beach. There's just
too much noise and chlorine and not enough fresh air. Outdoor
pools can be okay, although a natural environment is best.

This is a warm weather version, so if the water's too cold for
swimming where you are, dress warmly and just imagine that you
are swimming in tropical waters. I've written this for beside the
ocean, since that's where I live, but you could also do this at a lake
or beside a river.

Lie on your back on the beach for a few minutes, with your
eyes closed, and feel the sand cradling you. Feel the warmth of the
sun on your face and body. Allow your weight to fall deep into the
earth. Allow your thoughts to drift away on the breeze (or melt
away in the sun) until you are completely relaxed and your mind
is empty. Fall asleep for a little while, if that's what you need to do.

When you are ready, open your eyes and move to a sitting position with your knees up so the soles of your bare feet are against
the sand. Place the palms of your hands against the sand beside
your hips. Feel the energy of the earth flowing through your body
through these contact points, and allow it to balance and recharge
you. Watch the waves roll in, and feel the energy of the ocean flow
into you.

Now walk into the water, and feel it embrace you.

Float in the water, and feel your weightlessness. Imagine that
you are back in the womb, with no cares, no thoughts, no worries,
no responsibilities. Feel the rhythm of the swell as it lifts you up
and down.

Dive under the surface at least once, so that the water touches
your entire body.

Feel the ocean swell carry you. Let the water wash you clean, and emerge from the ocean feeling clean and renewed.

Walk on the beach, either along the water's edge or in the dry sand. Do a walking meditation, focusing on the movement of your feet. Walking on the beach can be almost as relaxing as a good foot massage, but it doesn't work as well if you don't pay complete attention!

Throughout either of these meditations, if you feel an emotion well up—anger, sadness, fear, regret, loneliness—don't try to fight or repress it. Allow it to be there. Whatever you feel in this moment is completely appropriate.

Try not to get distracted into thinking about someone, or re-playing scenes in your mind. Simply witness what you are feeling, and acknowledge it. Return your attention to the present, to your senses. Keep breathing. If you are swimming, stay relaxed. If you are walking, keep walking. Slow down. Focus on your breath.

Follow these meditations with some journal work—either while still at the park or beach, or later the same day.

Creating a Sense of Security

You may be feeling emotionally or physically vulnerable during the Centering phase. Here are some feng shui things you can do to create a greater feeling of security in your home or bedroom.

SLEEP IN THE BACK HALF OF THE HOUSE

Take out your floor plan, and draw a line through the midpoint of the home, halfway between the front and back of the house. Is your bedroom in front of or in back of this line?

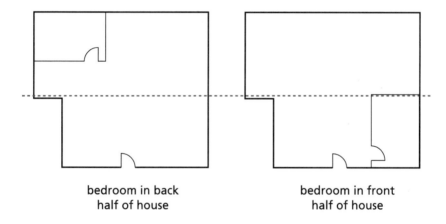

bedroom in back
half of house

bedroom in front
half of house

A bedroom that is in the back half of the home helps you feel more secure and in control. It's like being in the command position (next page) relative to the entire house or apartment. The back of the house is also usually quieter and more private—well-suited to a bedroom.

The front of the house is usually closer to the street, more exposed to noise from traffic and the light from car headlights at night. Energetically, it is a less secure and protected space, and therefore not ideal for a bedroom.

PLACE YOUR BED IN THE "COMMAND POSITION"

In feng shui, we want major pieces of furniture to be positioned so that they give you a view of the doorway, preferably with a solid wall behind you for support, and off to one side so you are not directly in the path of *chi* coming in the door.

This is called the command position, and it will put you more securely in command of your life. One of the most important adjustments you can make to your bedroom is to place your bed in the command position.

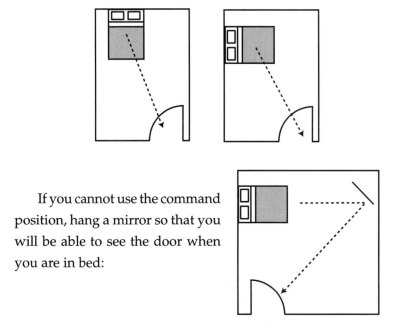

If you cannot use the command position, hang a mirror so that you will be able to see the door when you are in bed:

PROTECT YOUR BEDROOM FROM SHA CHI

Look out your bedroom windows. What do you see? If there is a road, utility tower, or any kind of ugly structure or sharp angle pointing directly at your bedroom, it's bombarding you with *sha* (negative) *chi*. If your bedroom has an exterior wall with no window, go outside and check for *sha chi* pointed at you.

If there's negative *chi* aimed
at your bedroom, place a *ba gua*
mirror on the exterior of the house
where it will deflect negative energy. A *ba gua* mirror is a small
round mirror set in an octagonal
red frame that is printed with the
eight *ba gua* trigrams.

These mirrors are only to be
used on the exterior of the house,
and should be hung with the trigram of three solid lines at the top.
Ba gua mirrors are available from most feng shui suppliers (see the
Resources section in the back of the book).

FU DOGS

Fu dogs are a traditional Chinese symbol of protection. These guardian symbols come in pairs, so make sure you have a matching set
of two: one fu dog alone will not be effective.

Place large fu dogs on either side of your front door. Empower
them to protect you and your home and to prevent unwanted
people from entering the house. Little fu dogs can be placed on a
table or shelf in your entryway or anywhere near the front door, or
you can place them in your bedroom.

OTHER GUARDIAN FIGURES

Buddhas, saints, angel figures or other images can also be empowered to bless and protect the home. Many cultures have traditional
guardian figures you could use at or near the front door.

FIRECRACKERS

Five firecrackers placed above your front door are a powerful symbol of protection. If you don't have real firecrackers, large fake ones made specifically to be used in this way are available in your city's Chinatown or from one of the feng shui suppliers listed in the Resources section or at www.fastfengshui.com.

PROTECT THE BACK DOOR

It is considered good in feng shui to have more than one door to the home, as this helps the *chi* to circulate more freely. However, a back door located in a relationship power spot could be weakening the *chi* of that area and creating a feeling of vulnerability.

Place one of the previously mentioned protection symbols just outside or inside the back door, or hang a bamboo flute horizontally above the door (on the inside of the house), with the mouthpiece toward the hinge side of the door.

Empower the flute to act like a sword, poised to cut off any negative energy before it can enter. If you happen to have a real sword lying around the house, you can use that instead of a bamboo flute. Hang it above the door so the hilt end of the sword is toward the hinge side of the door and the sharp edge of the blade is pointed down. A sharp kitchen knife can also be used. Tie a red tassel to it, for extra power.

WIND CHIMES

Another way to deflect negative *chi* coming toward the house is to hang a wind chime on the outside of the house where it will be in line with the source of *sha chi*. You can also hang a wind chime at your back door for protection. Make sure the sound of the chime will not disturb you at night while you're trying to sleep.

BELLS

A bedroom that is behind the front door is vulnerable in feng shui terms because it is not in the command position in the house. A bedroom is "behind" the front door when the back of the door faces the bedroom location when the door is open. Still not clear? Perhaps another diagram will help:

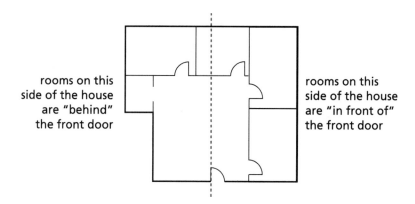

rooms on this side of the house are "behind" the front door

rooms on this side of the house are "in front of" the front door

One of the most common goofs people make when they draw up their floor plan is not paying attention to which way the doors open. If you're checking your floor plan right now to assess your bedroom location, I recommend that you physically walk over to your front door and make absolutely sure that you've drawn it correctly on the floor plan. You'd be amazed how many times I've seen this done backwards.

The cure for this situation, should you discover that you have it, is to hang a brass bell on the front door, so it rings when the door is opened. Traditionally, a shop-keeper's bell is used. This is a bell on a spring that jingles when the door is opened. I tried this in my previous apartment and found the the sound too jangly and annoying. Irritating cures are not good feng shui, so I replaced the bell with a wind chime, which I hung so that the door hit the dangly part as it opened and rang the chimes. You could do the same.

Your Private Sanctuary

One of the nicest things you can do for yourself during Centering is to find or create a private, secure space where you can be peaceful and alone. Often this will be a corner of your bedroom, although you may have an even better spot available to you.

Here are some things you may wish to consider as you select and arrange an appropriate area in your home. Keep in mind that these are general guidelines—it's fine if your ideal spot doesn't fit all (or even many) of these criteria.

POWER SPOTS

Check your floor plan for the location of your relationship and Centering power spots. Is there a place in any of those power spots that is a potential location for your personal sanctuary?

Look at *ken gua* (self-understanding), as well; it is associated with meditation and spirituality, so it's a good place for retreating from the world for a little while.

PRIVACY

Look for a place where you can close a door, draw a curtain, or just be out of sight and undisturbed for half an hour or so every day. This could be a personal corner, or a more public place in the house that you will have to yourself at certain times of the day.

LUXURY

Make your sanctuary cozy and comfortable. Get out your journal or a piece of paper, and make a list of at least nine words that mean "luxury" to you. Your personal luxury doesn't have to be expensive. It might include:

- Soft fabrics such as velvets and chenilles

- Fancy throw pillows with brocade trim

- Beautiful writing paper and a fine fountain pen

- An orchid in full bloom

- Your favorite slippers

- A cashmere sweater

- A place to smoke where no one will complain or chastise you (I'd rather you quit, but your luxury is your choice)

- Expensive perfume

- Time to sit and sip a glass of wine

- Fragranced candles

- Beautiful artwork

Anything that you particularly enjoy pampering yourself with counts as a luxury, even if it's something plain and simple. Incorporate at least three of these things in your sanctuary.

A PLACE TO SIT

Your sanctuary is the place for your favorite comfy chair. If your chair is less than new, cover it with a piece of fabric, or have a slipcover made for it. Ratty old upholstery brings ratty old *chi* into this important spot, regardless of how comfortable the chair is.

If it's been around for a really long time, or is second hand, smudge your chair with sage or incense to get rid of old *chi*. You could also toss nine pieces of fresh orange peel on the arms, back and seat, empower them to absorb and remove stale energy, and leave them overnight.

A BEAUTIFUL VIEW

In feng shui terms, ugliness is *sha* (negative) *chi*. Things that are graceful and pleasing to the eye have good *chi*. As you relax in your sanctuary, make sure that what you look at is beautiful and soothing. If you have a beautiful landscape view, soak up its good *chi* with your eyes and spirit. You may even make a corner of your garden into your personal sanctuary.

Place a beautiful print, painting, or poster on the wall of an indoor sanctuary. If there's a window in your sanctuary, do you see something pleasant through it? If not, a sheer curtain softens the view while still allowing light through. Or, you can cover the window with a pretty shade or a plain window shade covered with attractive fabric.

IMPORTANT PEOPLE

Images or photographs of people who are important to you are a nice addition to your sanctuary. Pictures of grandparents remind you of where you came from, and photos of your kids connect you with what is to come. Good friends belong here, too, along with spiritual leaders and inspirational figures of all kinds.

A PICTURE OF YOU

If you are reinventing yourself during this time, have a new photograph taken of yourself, and place it in your sanctuary. Don't use picture of yourself that dates from your previous relationship or earlier. You want to display (and see) who you are right now.

REFLECTION

A mirror in your sanctuary symbolizes insight and clarity. If you can see yourself in the mirror while you are seated in your comfy chair, make sure that you see your entire face. If just part of your head is visible, it could have a negative effect on your self-image.

ILLUMINATION

Make sure your sanctuary has appropriate lighting. This could be as simple as the morning sun shining in the window while you do your yoga or meditation, or you may need a reading lamp for writing in your journal before bed at night.

Light symbolizes understanding and recognition. It should be neither too soft nor too bright; what that means in terms of bulb type and wattage depends on the room and time of day you use it.

A KEY IMAGE

Your private sanctuary is a wonderful place to keep an image that has important symbolic meaning for you. This could be a photograph, painting, piece of sculpture or other art.

YOUR COLLAGE

If you've made a collage of where you want to go and what you'd like to get out of life, display it here. If you haven't made a collage yet, you'll have the opportunity to make one in Phase 2.

PLANTS OR FLOWERS

Include fresh plants or flowers if you can, so you can benefit from their positive energy. If you have the black thumb of death when it comes to houseplants, a life-like artificial plant or floral arrangement will do. Avoid dried flowers, which have no living *chi* left in them. If you adorn your sanctuary with beautiful fresh flowers, be absolutely vigilant about changing the water daily and removing old blossoms as soon as they start to wilt.

FRAGRANCE

Have something in your sanctuary that smells just wonderful to you. You might want to keep a small bottle of your favorite scent in your private nook, and dab a little on each time you retreat there. Flowers, candles, and sachets are other possibilities. Chances are your sanctuary will be a small, cozy place, so be careful not to overdo it.

FRESH AIR

An open window in the next room will do, so long as the fresh air gets to you. Stale, stagnant air is a sign of stale, stagnant *chi*, and that's not what we want here. Besides, a little fresh air will help prevent all those scented candles and flowers from giving you a headache—even in feng shui you can have too much of a good thing!

So, now that you've created your sanctuary, what do you do there? How about: sit, relax, be nice to yourself. Make a cup of tea, and spend a few minutes with that novel you've been wanting to read. Meditation is good, as is journal work, creative writing, or just savoring some quiet time alone.

One more important guideline: absolutely, positively no work-related stuff or TV in your sanctuary! (I hope I didn't need to tell you that.) Soothing music is good; talk radio and the news are out. This is where you go to be you, so shut out the outside world for a little while and center yourself here in your private spot.

Moving On

As you become more fully grounded in the present and deepen your understanding of who you are and what you need, you'll move out of the Centering phase of the Relationship Cycle and discover that you are ready to emerge from your nest and explore the world of dating again.

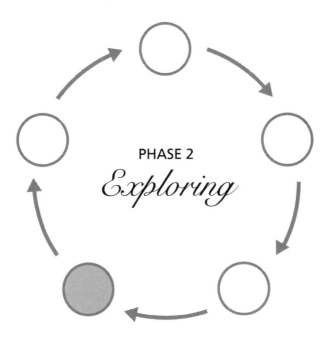

PHASE 2

Exploring

The second stage in your journey through the Relationship Cycle is Exploring. You feel stronger and more centered now, after the work of Phase 1, and are ready to jump back into the pool and see if you remember how to swim.

This is the time when you get serious about dating again, even if you're not yet ready for a serious relationship. When you make the shift to becoming more outwardly focused after the inward focus of the Centering phase, Exploring offers strategies and tips for jump-starting your social life and expanding your network of friends.

Your tasks for the Exploring stage are to create space in your home for new energy to come in and to activate and expand your social network. When you focus on meeting a wide range of people, you increase your odds of connecting with the perfect partner you've been waiting for.

This is also a great time to expand your horizons in whatever ways appeal to you: take up a new hobby, enroll in a class, get involved with a local charitable organization, visit a new place, go on a cruise, or just explore your own neighborhood and city.

Keep in mind that you won't meet people sitting at home, so make sure your activities get you out of the house and into the company of others!

The Water Element in Feng Shui

The Exploring phase is associated with the WATER element in feng shui. We can gain a greater understanding of the qualities and objectives of this stage by taking a look at the meanings and characteristics of water.

Water is reviving, nurturing, clean, pure, calming, soothing. We can swim in a lake, soak in a hot bath or take a cool refreshing shower, or get happily soaked to the skin in a warm summer rain. Water can also sweep us away in a flash flood or tidal wave, and it will wear down a mountain over time. For every gentle summer shower, there's bitter November sleet; water can chill us to the bone as well as soothe our aches and pains at the end of a long day.

Symbolically, water is often associated with our emotions and subconscious selves, and is regarded as a source of vitality. It can signify potential that is not yet manifest.

THE FENG SHUI VIEW OF WATER

In feng shui, the WATER element is associated with the season of winter, when the *chi* of the earth begins to shift toward spring. Although the weather may be cold, the transition to warmer times is just ahead. As snow and ice begin to melt in late winter, water trickles and flows and life returns.

In Traditional Chinese Medicine, WATER is associated with the kidneys and bladder. Feng shui also associates WATER with the birth canal as the channel through which we emerge into the world.

The emotion affected by WATER imbalance is fear. It is in the Exploring state of the Relationship Cycle that confronting fear and finding the courage to go out into the world and look for love again (instead of staying in the safety and security of home) is most likely to be an issue. The sound associated with WATER is "groaning," which may be what you do when you think about having to start dating again. Go ahead and groan if it makes you feel better; by the end of this phase you'll agree it was worth it.

Feng shui distinguishes between two types of WATER: still and moving.

- **Still water** symbolizes wisdom, clarity and deep understanding. When this energy is strong in you, you have a broad and sound perspective on life, and your judgment is sharp and clear. When this energy is weak, you might make poor decisions because your judgment is not good. Lack of clarity leads to arguments, and your words or behavior may seem hypocritical.

- **Moving water** is associated with prosperity, career, and—most important for your love life—social connections. Think of moving water as representing the ocean of people that you swim in. When moving water *chi* is strong, you go out a lot, travel frequently, make lots of new contacts, meet people easily, and are on the phone a lot. This can be exhausting, but you should be feeling rested after the Centering phase, and Exploring is definitely the time to put on your dancing shoes and go out on the town. When moving water is weak, on the other hand, you may find you are home most of the time, and don't have a large circle of friends. This chapter will tell you how to fix that.

JOURNALING

Find some quiet time to explore your personal experience of the WATER relationship phase. What insights have you gained from exploring WATER energy from a feng shui perspective? How have you reacted to the challenges and opportunities of Exploring as you moved through this phase in the past?

- How do you usually respond to this phase, both emotionally and physically?

- What aspects of becoming more social and meeting new people are easy for you? Which are difficult?

- What do you most look forward to about this stage? What makes you "groan"?

Think about what personal challenges are likely to surface for you in this phase of the Relationship Cycle. This might include:

- Making yourself focus on what you need to do in your home, when it's so much more fun to go out

- Finding the courage to go out, if you are shy and would rather stay home and work on your clutter

- Paying more attention to your appearance, so you always make a good first impression

- Handling how your children react when you start dating again

- Restructuring your budget so you can invest in the services of a baby sitter, professional organizer, personal trainer, image consultant, dating service, or whatever other outside help you may need

Water Energy and the Ba Gua

The WATER element is associated with *kan gua* (career, wisdom, and social connections). *Kan* is located at the center of the lower side of the *ba gua*. If the front entry to your home is in *kan gua*, that will be an especially important power spot for you during the Exploring phase.

kan
career,
social connections

If you are placing the *ba gua* according to the compass directions, *kan gua* is in the north.

From the perspective of the challenges and tasks of Exploring, *kan gua* supports activating your social life and creating new opportunities.

Because the element of *kan gua* is WATER, METAL-type cures and colors are appropriate here, as are all kinds of WATER cures.* Avoid placing too much WOOD energy in this *gua*, as it will drink up the WATER, unless you also add METAL to support WATER. Remember, too, that EARTH can muddy or clog WATER unless you also add METAL to create a three-element arc of the creative cycle.

YOUR EXPLORING BA GUA

Draw a nine-square *ba gua* grid in your notebook or on a blank sheet of paper (or photocopy the *ba gua* template on page 204). Write "Exploring" in the middle (*tai chi*) square.

Start with *kan gua*—the square on the middle of the bottom row. Write in "social life" or any other specific meaning this area

---

* You can find information about the cycles of the elements and about specific feng shui cures and objects in the Appendices at the back of the book.

may have for you, based on your personal issues and goals for the Exploring phase.

Now, think about the other *guas* (refer to the *ba gua* map on page 188, if necessary), and identify any personal meanings they may have for you in the Exploring stage. It's okay if you don't feel a strong connection between a specific *gua* and your needs and experiences right now. Focus on the areas that do resonate with you, and note their meanings on your Exploring *ba gua*.

Below is an example of the *ba gua* from the perspective of the Exploring phase. Remember that there are no right or wrong answers; this is your *ba gua*, based on your feelings, and it's okay to leave some areas blank.

what I have to offer in a relationship	image consultant?	
	EXPLORING	be creative about places to meet people
don't let being shy stop me	Network!	dating services

The final step in this exercise is to choose which *guas* will be your top priorities for the Exploring phase. For example, if you are feeling shy and not as self-confident as you'd like going into this phase, you can work with *hsun gua* (fortunate blessings) to become more aware of what you have to offer to others, and with *li gua* (fame and reputation) to help others recognize you for the bright, charming, interesting person that you really are.

Your close friends and relatives may be thrilled that you've decided it's time to start dating again—or they might be less supportive than you'd like, making *jen gua* (family) important for you now.

Chien gua (helpful friends) is also a good area for feng shui during the Exploring phase, because it can help you hook up with the right baby sitter, personal coach, or dating service.

Use your personal *ba gua* to help you fine-tune your affirmations and visualizations during this phase.

Find Your Exploring Power Spots

Yes, once again we're going to fine-tune your power spots. This time you will compare the location of your relationship power spots with the key *guas* that you've decided deserve some attention during the Exploring phase.

First, look to see if *kan gua* (social connections) of your home, bedroom, personal sanctuary* or other key room overlaps with any of your relationship power spots. If you decided any other *guas* were especially important for you now, look for overlaps with those areas as well. For example, if your bedroom is in *li gua* (reputation) of the house, all of your bedroom power spots will help you make a good impression on others.

If you are using the *ba gua* according to the entry, also take a look at the compass directions. Are any of your relationship power spots in the northern sector of your home or of that room?

You may find lots of overlap areas, or none. If you don't find any areas of overlap, focus your feng efforts first on *kan gua* and your front door, and then apply the guidelines in this chapter to other power spots throughout the house. As we go along, you'll learn lots of ways to increase your social activity and how to use the energy of moving water to activate *kan gua*.

The rest of this chapter details specific things you can do to enhance the Exploring phase. As always, pay attention to your intuition as you decide which of these tips are right for you. As you activate your social life, it will be especially important to reserve some quiet time for yourself, so you can stay in touch with your feelings and record your insights in your feng shui journal.

---

* See pages 88-92 in the Centering chapter.

Feng Shui for the Exploring Phase

Make Room for New Experiences

The most sure-fire way to make it difficult to meet anybody new is to keep your house bursting at the seams with stuff—especially stuff that binds you energetically to your previous relationships. If your love life needs a breath of fresh air, start by giving yourself and your house some breathing room.

We touched on this earlier in the book, but it's important enough to repeat at least once more: if you want to bring a new relationship into your life, you'll need to make room for it. For some people, that work may be mostly on an emotional level, and a lot of the clearing out of the detritus of a past relationship will have been accomplished in the Centering phase. For others, the big problem is dealing with a house full of stuff. Now that you're in the Exploring phase, it's time to get serious about creating space for the new things you'd like to welcome into your life. Here are some ways you can do that.

TAKE A SPACE-O-METER READING OF YOUR HOME

"A space-o-what?," you ask. Okay, I admit, there's no such thing as a space-o-meter—it's what I call the method I use to do a quick assessment of the scale of a client's storage and clutter problem. It requires taking an objective look at things that you may not even notice on a day-to-day basis, so having a friend do this with you can be a revealing exercise. It's helpful to have a copy of your floor plan available as you assess your clutter, so get one out now, and take a look at each room in your house.

When I'm working with a client, I like to start in the front hall, but you can begin anywhere. Stand in the doorway of any room, and look around as though this is the first time you've ever been in there. Here's what I want you to look for:

- Flat surfaces such as end tables, coffee tables, dresser tops, and counters

- Bookcases or other shelving

- Cupboards, cabinets and (if you're in the kitchen) the refrigerator and freezer

- Dressers, chests, file cabinets or other storage

- Trash cans and wastebaskets

- Recycling bins and laundry hampers

Now, here's the scary (oops, I mean fun) part. I want you to rate the "saturation point" of the room on a scale of 1-10, where 1 is like a hotel room (empty drawers, clear surfaces, etc.) and 10 is if there is absolutely positively no place left to put one more thing. Imagine that you have just arrived home from the mall or supermarket, laden with shopping bags, and now you have to put your new things away. Where will they go?

Some of this you'll be able to do just by looking, but anything with a lid, door, drawer, or "open mouth" (like a wastebasket) will need to be peered into.

Okay, what's your score? That bad, huh. Don't give up yet, 'cause it's about to get worse! Award this room 1 extra point for *each* of the following conditions that apply:

- There is anything at all on top of the TV or stereo

- There are loose CDs or audiotapes lying around not in their cases

- There is anything other than throw pillows or a lap blanket on any chair or the couch—*and*, you get a demerit point if the blanket is in a wrinkled heap instead of neatly folded

- Books are stacked more than one volume deep on any shelf

- There are more than three magazines or books on the coffee table (or equivalent piece of furniture) per adult resident

- There is anything "filed" on the floor around your desk, couch, or favorite comfy chair

- The wastebasket or laundry hamper is piled high or literally overflowing

- There are clean clothes lying around waiting to be put away

I could probably go on, but I'm guessing you'd rather I stopped here. Anybody get a "perfect 20" yet?

Hang in just a little longer, because there's one more step (do I hear that groaning sound again?): if there is a closet in or adjoining that room, open up the closet door and rate that space, too. On a scale of 1 to 10 (1 being empty, 10 being "run-for-your-life-it's-about-to-blow"), how full of stuff is your closet?

Note the scores for the room and the closet on your floor plan.

Now, if you can stand it, do the same for the rest of your house. You may—if you truly believe this room is no better or worse than the rest of your house—use the score for this first room for the entire house. You may also omit from your assessment any of your children's rooms if they are responsible for keeping that space tidy; I will not hold you responsible for your 15-year-old's space.

Don't be overly alarmed if your home has gone off the high end of the space-o-meter scale. You are in good company, I assure you. If your base score was 8 or under for most rooms, and you averaged 3 or fewer demerit points per room, you're doing well.

If you are patting yourself on the back for achieving a score of 6 or 7, with no demerit points, for most of the rooms in your house, I'll be curious to know what your closet scores are. I have been in more than one seemingly immaculate home where the closets have been crammed full, every square inch of every shelf, up to the ceiling and flush with the door.

GO ON A CLUTTER-HUNT

With a copy of your floor plan in hand (you can use the same one you just used for the space-o-meter activity), grab a highlighter or colored pencil, walk through your entire home, noting on your floor plan every accumulation of clutter you find. Pay special attention to any clutter in your romance or Exploring power spots, and circle those areas for priority attention! If you are not sure whether or not something is "clutter" or not, follow these basic guidelines:

Books, CDs, and videotapes

A few books on the bedside table are not clutter if you are actively reading them at least every few days. That pile of paperbacks you read years ago and haven't looked at since is clutter. Give them to your local library.

Music you listen to from time to time is fine, as are videotapes that you actually watch. CDs and tapes you haven't played in three years are ready to go.

Clothes

Clothes you love and wear—even if only for special occasions—are not clutter. Clothes you haven't worn in years, or that you plan to wear when you lose weight, are clutter. If you want to keep one "skinny" outfit around as an incentive, fine, but how many of your clothes really fit you right now?

Multiples of things

How many of any one thing do you really need? I'm not talking about things that you collect as a hobby, but about that bin under the kitchen sink with all the paper grocery bags in it. Sure, they come in handy, but if the ones on the bottom have been there for a year, you're holding on to way too many of them.

Multiples lurk in all kinds of places, and come in all kinds of forms. How many tablecloths do you really need and use? How many sets of workout clothes and water bottles? How many extra sheets and towels? How many bottles of body lotion, shampoo, or nail polish? How many pens and pencils on your desk? How many magazine subscriptions? Get the picture?

"Just in case" things

Stuff that you are keeping because you might need it "some day" is almost always clutter. It is tremendously liberating to trust that you will always be able to obtain what you need. Clearing out all that "someday" stuff creates space—literally and symbolically—for new experiences to come in.

MAKE A "LOVE MAP"

A "love map" is a collage of what you are going to be making room for as you clear out your stuff. This is fun, and will help you sort through all those magazines that have been piling up.

Those of you who have read the first Fast Feng Shui book may have already made a collage. This one is specifically for your love life. Use a piece of posterboard as a backing, or use a letter-size manila folder for a portable collage: open, it will stand up on a desk or shelf, and it's a good size to carry with you in your tote bag or briefcase. If you can find a red folder, that's even better (red is the feng shui power color, and it's good for relationship energy, too). You'll also need a glue-stick or two, and scissors.

Start with a big stack of magazines, the more pictures and bold headlines and full-page ads the better. Tear or cut out images, words, and phrases that reflect the people and experiences you want to attract into your love life.

Pictures of men or women whom you find sexy or appealing are a good start, as are any images that reflect how you want to feel in your ideal romance, places you'd like the two of you to go, and things you'd like to do together. Romantic dinners, exotic vacations, hiking a mountain trail, just cooking dinner together at home or pushing your kids in a swing at the park—choose images or words that capture aspects of the life you want to live with your future love. It's a good idea to do your cutting first, and then paste up words and images as a separate step. If you paste as you go along, you're liable to run out of room for even better images you come across deeper in your magazine pile.

It's very important to be loose and intuitive during the collage making process. If a picture appeals to you, tear it out, even if you're not sure why at the moment.

The first time I did this was in Michelle Passoff's* clutter-clearing workshop, which I attended in order to better advise my feng

* This clutter guru has a book out, too, *Lighten Up! Free Yourself from Clutter*. See the Resources section in the back of the book, or visit www.fastfengshui.com for a link to her site.

shui clients on dealing with their own clutter. And yes, I hoped to benefit personally, too! Without planning it, I found myself cutting out large letters to spell the word "whimsy," which became the center of the collage. The collage helped me realize that I needed more spontaneous fun in my life. I was very busy with corporate projects, my feng shui practice, two writer's groups and so on, and taking no time for myself. What I most needed to clear out was some of the *time* clutter—and this exercise helped me realize that I needed to create time as well as space for a relationship to happen.

When you allow your collage to grow intuitively, you allow your inner wisdom to make itself visible to you. Pay attention to those messages, even if at first they don't seem to have anything to do with relationships.

A collage is especially powerful if there's an image of you in it, so dig out a couple of snapshots of yourself and photocopy them in several sizes, so you'll have a selection to choose from. Now grab that glue stick and add a picture of you to your collage right next to the guy or girl of your dreams.

Place your collage in one of your romance or Exploring power spots, where you will see it frequently. When you look at your "love map" every day, the images will have an energetic effect on you on a subconscious level. This daily reinforcement will help you to keep your goals in mind and to manifest what you are seeking. As you tackle your clutter, keep your focus on what you are making room for in your life.

THE CLUTTER-BUSTER'S MANTRA

"Love it, Use it, or Lose it!"

If you've read the first Fast Feng Shui book, you will already know these important words to live by (and you *have* been living by them, right?).

When you can't decide what to do with something, ask yourself: Do I *love* it? Do I *use* it? Do I really *need* it? If your answer to any question is "yes," you get to keep it. If you answer "no" to all three questions, out it goes.

"But, but, but...," I hear you say. Okay, some things are hard to let go of. Remind yourself that keeping something just because you think you might, maybe, possibly miss or need it someday is a recipe for clutter. Take a deep breath and go look at your collage for a moment. Now think about the item in question: is it something you want or need to carry with you into your new life, or is it something you can get rid of to make room for what you really want?

KEEP A MIGHT-BE-TREASURE CHEST

Letting go of things that you've had for a long time can be difficult. *Chachkas*—small, useless-but-pretty objects that arrive in our homes as gifts or impulse purchases—often go through a multi-step process before leaving the premises. The transition from "Ohmigod, I love it!" to "I can get rid of *this!*" goes something like this: coffee table (3-6 months), shelf (1-2 years), closet shelf (1 year), deep in the closet or out in the garage (1 year), out the door.

With a little conscious effort, you can speed this process up. If you just can't make up your mind about whether or not to get rid of something, put it in a box along with the other things you can't decide about. I strongly suggest you try to limit this stash to just *one* box, as difficult as that may be. Now close the box up and find some out-of-the-way place to keep it—like the back of a closet, if you've cleaned out enough stuff so there's room in there.

Get out your calendar or agenda book, and pick a date roughly a year from now. Make a note in your calendar on that date to evaluate the contents of your "might-be-treasure" chest.

When that future date arrives, take a few minutes before opening the box to make a list of everything you can remember putting into it. Then open the box up and see what you find. Chances are good that any item you'd forgotten about can now be released from your life, as can anything you haven't missed, needed, or wanted in the past twelve months.

QUICK CLUTTER TIP #1

If you have a major clutter problem, and not enough time to deal with it, here's a quick way to get started. Go to each of your romance and Exploring power spots and remove at least three pieces of clutter from each one.

Do this all at once: do not stop to answer the phone, take out the trash, have a cup of tea, or read that magazine you just came across. This won't take long, but do make sure you'll have enough uninterrupted time to get to each power spots in one session.

Now, get out your calendar and make sure you schedule some time—even a few minutes a day is better than nothing—to keep the clutter-clearing effort going.

QUICK CLUTTER TIP #2

If you're really having trouble getting started on your clutter, use this method from the space clearing process outlined in Phase 1. In space clearing, sound vibration is used to shake up stuck energy. You can loosen up your clutter by briskly clapping your hands over it, ringing a bell over it, or hanging a wind chime over it.

It helps to keep a strong intention in your mind and heart as you do this that the sound waves will start loosening up that stuck energy.

QUICK CLUTTER TIP #3

Return everything you have borrowed from someone else. If you've had it for so long you've been hoping they just forgot about it, that's a burden of shame and guilt you're piling on yourself. Surely you don't need that, any more than you desperately need whatever you borrowed.

Chances are your friend will think better of you for returning it embarrassingly late than if you don't return it at all.

QUICK CLUTTER TIP #4

Planning to give the things you no longer want or need to a local charity is just a start. You don't get clutter-clearing credit until the stuff is actually out of the house! Pack those things up and load them into the car and drop them off—or arrange for them to be picked up. Otherwise all you have done is organize your clutter.

MOVE THINGS AROUND

This tip is for those rare folks who don't have a clutter poblem. (If you've been clearing a lot of clutter, you'll have already done this one along the way.) When you live by the neatnik rule, "a place for everything and everything in its place," your home may be admirably tidy, but it could also be rather static.

When your things stay in same place for a long time, the energy around them can get stuck, and you may start feeling as though your life is stuck, too. One of the easiest ways to create an energy shift in your life is to move things around in your home. Rearranging your furniture can have a big impact, as it may dramatically improve the flow of *chi* through your home.

You don't have to be that ambitious, however. Moving little things from their accustomed positions is also effective, and becomes more so if you do it in one of these three ways:

- Look around your home and move 36 things that have been in exactly the same place for at least six months.

- Go to each room of your home, and move 9 things that have been in the exact same spot for at least six months.

- Go to each of your Exploring power spots and move 9 things that have been putting down roots there for at least six months.

Whichever of these methods you choose, be sure to use the body-speech-mind empowerment process (pages 10-12). This is a good time to use the dispelling mudra version to help shake the stuck energy loose.

Welcome Change and Opportunties

Congratulations! You've cleared out your clutter (or are making steady progress in that area), and have a clear idea of what you are creating space for in your life. The next step is to identify and fix anything that could be preventing a healthy flow of new energy and opportunities from getting into your home, or that might be hindering your ability to meet and connect with people.

OPEN THE DOOR

As you now know, your front door is called the "mouth of *chi*" because it is the most important way for new energy to get into your home. When your front door and entryway are blocked in any way, fresh *chi* and new opportunties have a hard time getting to you. The main entry to your home carries much of the same energy as *kan gua* (social connections), regardless of where it is on the *ba gua*.

Your home's "mouth of *chi*" should definitely be on your list of Exploring power spots, and should be a priority area for clutter-clearing efforts. Make sure that:

- The door opens and closes easily and completely

- The front stoop, porch, or hallway is clean, tidy, well-lit, and free of clutter

USE YOUR FRONT DOOR

When you go in and out of your house through the garage all the time, instead of using the front door, you are not taking advantage of the beneficial *chi* associated with the main entryway. Make an effort to use your front door more often, and you will be activating that important area of your home.

FOCUS ON CREATING OPPORTUNITIES

Every time you leave your house or apartment, you are creating an opportunity to connect with someone new. *Every* time. You can use the body-speech-mind empowerment process to make stepping through your front door a feng shui ritual:

- Pause for a moment before you leave the house, and make an affirmation such as, "My day is filled with opportunities to meet someone new," or "As I step out this door I move closer to meeting my partner," or whatever works for you.

- Visualize meeting a new romantic prospect today. Since you don't know what the specific circumstances will be, focus on imagining that first rush of excitement and possibility.

- With your heart filled with anticipation, reach out and open the door and take that step forward to meeting someone special.

OPEN UP A BLOCKED ENTRYWAY

What do you see when you enter your front door? If there is a wall less than six feet in front of you, it may be blocking your ability to move forward and connect with people. The best solution for this is to put a large mirror on that wall:

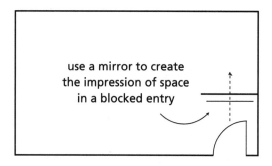

use a mirror to create
the impression of space
in a blocked entry

Some feng shui experts feel that a mirror directly opposite the door will bounce the *chi* right back out again. In my opinion this will depend on the specific circumstances of your entryway, and on what is reflected in the mirror. It is just as likely that the mirror will expand and brighten the space, and draw more positive energy in. Try a mirror, and see how it feels.

If you don't want to place a mirror in your entry, or it just doesn't look right with your décor, another solution is to hang a landscape painting or photograph in the place where a mirror would go. The image should be large and have a distant horizon; this will visually open up the space and allow you to "see" into the distance.

OPEN UP A PINCHED NOSE ENTRY

A similar problem, the "pinched nose" entry, occurs when the front door opens onto a very narrow hallway. This is thought to restrict the flow of *chi* and opportunities into the home. A pinched nose entry can be corrected by mirroring the wall onto which the door opens.

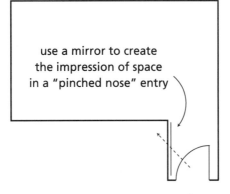

use a mirror to create
the impression of space
in a "pinched nose" entry

USE A MIRROR TO ENHANCE THE ENTRY

Mirrors are not just for problem entries. Even if your entryway is spacious, you can hang a large mirror there and empower it to enhance and expand your opportuntities and social contacts. And when you have a mirror near the front door, you can check your appearance before you go out, to help ensure you make a good first impression on everyone you meet today.

BEAUTIFY THE ENTRY WITH PLANTS AND FLOWERS

Outside on your stoop, steps, or porch, pots of brightly flowering plants help to attract positive *chi* to your home. Indoors, lush green plants, a blossoming orchid, or a bouquet of fresh flowers bring vibrant natural *chi* into your home and enhance the energy of your entryway.

If your front door is in *kan gua* (career, social contacts), keep in mind that lots of plants will absorb the WATER *chi* of that space. Be sure to add a water fountain and some METAL energy as well, to support the WATER energy of *kan gua*.

ACTIVATE KAN GUA WITH MOVING WATER

Moving water, such as a water fountain, brings prosperity and good luck to the home, and is a powerful enhancer for *kan gua* or for your main entryway.

If your fountain features a stream of water that flows down only on one side, make sure you place it so the water is flowing toward your home, not away from it. (If your fountain has an even flow of water all around, this is not an issue.)

Be sure also to keep a watchful eye on the water level; if it drops too low, the pump can be damaged. In a dry environment you may need to add more water as often as every day.

VIRTUAL WATER

If placing a water fountain in your entry or outside the front door is not practical, look for an image of a waterfall, river, or ocean waves to hang in the front hall of your home.

You could also purchase a wave machine, or a sound machine that you can set to play the sound of tropical rain, a bubbling brook, or ocean waves washing against the shore. Leave it on for as much of the day as your electric bill can support (best times: 11 AM - 1 PM and 11 PM - 1 AM), and empower it to activate the *chi* of *kan gua*.

ACTIVATE THE ENTRY WITH A FLAG OR BRIGHT LIGHT

A brightly colored flag or string of flags will activate the exterior of your home and attract positive *chi*. Hang it near your front door or in *kan gua* to help attract new social connections. If the light in or around your front door is dim, install another light there, or put higher-wattage bulbs in the existing fixtures.

PROTECT THE ENTRY

A wind chime hung near the front door on the outside of the house will deflect any negative *chi* aimed at the entry. You can also place a pair of fu dogs (see page 85) in your entry to protect the home. Empower both these cures to prevent any undesireable or inappropriate people from being attracted to you or your home.

Activate Your Network

A key strategy for activating your social life is to rejuvenate your existing network of social, business, and personal connections. Here are some ways to do that.

DRAW A NETWORK MAP

Take out a piece of paper (unlined is best), and a colored pencil or pen with red or bright pink lead or ink. In the center of the paper, draw a circle and write your initials in it.

Now think about all the different real or virtual communities you are a part of in both your professional and personal lives. Include extended family, friends from high school and college, school and community organizations in which you are active, the other regulars at your gym or yoga class, the members of your on-line discussion lists.*

Draw another circle for each group of people you know or are associated with in the space surrounding the circle that represents you. Now draw a connecting line from each of these other circles to you. Beside each circle, write the names of three people with whom you feel a personal connection. If you can't come up with specific names for a group or groups, that's okay. Just do the best you can.

If you are a perfectionist and your map is a mess by the time you're done, there's nothing to stop you from taking a clean sheet of paper and making a nice, neat final copy. It's not necessary though; the attention you put into thinking about and drawing all these connections is more important than how it looks.

---

* It doesn't matter that you haven't met these folks. I connected with the man I live with through a Chinese astrology discussion list on the Internet. He posted a question, I replied, and the rest, as they say, is history.

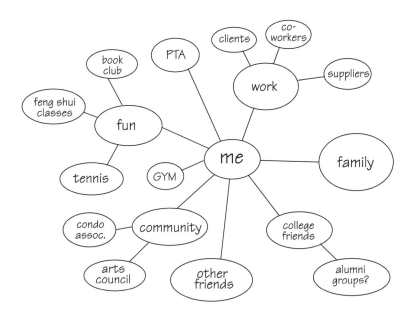

When your network map is done, take a moment to recognize the number of people that you already have a connection to, and to realize that any one of them might in some way help you connect to your next romantic partner.

Using the body-speech-mind empowerment method (pages 10-12), visualize a web of energy connecting you to all these people, and state your intention that each person-to-person connection be empowered to help you meet your next partner.

Place the network map in one of your Exploring or relationship power spots, and use the red power color in some way. For example, you could:

- Roll up the map and tie a 9" length of red ribbon around it

- Glue the map to a red backing, such as a red file folder

- Keep the map in a large red envelope

EMPOWER YOUR TELEPHONE

Here are some ways you can empower your telephone to help you connect with a new romantic partner:

- Place your phone in the relationship area (*kun gua*: back right corner) of your desk, bedroom dresser, or nightstand

- Place your phone in a relationship or Exploring power spot

- Buy a red (feng shui power color), pink (romance), or black or navy blue (WATER energy) phone

- Place a red, pink, black, or dark blue cloth underneath your telephone

- Hang a faceted crystal ball over your telephone to activate communication

- If you frequently use a cordless or cellular phone, make those calls from a relationship or Exploring power spot whenever possible

Remember to use the body-speech-mind empowerment process with any of these tactics you choose to use.

PICK UP THE PHONE

Here's a fun ritual you can do to activate your social life. Initiating contact with folks you already know stimulates the *chi* of your social life, making it easier for you to meet and connect with new people as well.

First, make a list of friends, relatives, and acquaintances with whom you have not spoken in at least six months. Go through your address book and holiday card list, or look at your network map for ideas. You'll need at least 27 names, plus a few extras to allow for folks who are travelling or hard to reach.

Although the guidelines for this ritual specify no *verbal* contact for six months, I recommend disqualifying anyone with whom you exchange frequent e-mail, even if you haven't had a voice conversation with that person in a long time. The idea is to activate dormant social connections, so keep your list focused on folks you haven't been in touch with at all lately.

There are two variations for this method: you can call three people a day for nine consecutive days, or call one person a day for 27 consecutive days. Make sure you will be able to keep up with this plan before you begin, because if you skip a day you will need to start all over again—and the folks you've already talked to will no longer meet that important "no voice contact in six months"qualification!

There are three requirements that you must follow for this cure to be effective:

1. You must actually *talk* to the person you call. Leaving a message on an answering machine does *not* count! This is why it's helpful to have a bunch of extra names on your list; it may take a few tries to catch up with some folks.

2. You cannot *complain* about anything during the entire conversation. That means you can't bitch and moan about your job or your ex or your weight or whatever. This is harder than it sounds! You have to really pay attention, and phrase everything positively.

3. You must say "yes" to all requests made of you, like it or not! "Let's get together for lunch next week," means you say, "That sounds great! Monday's good for me, if we can meet downtown." When your friend says, "I'm taking a great *tae bo* class on Tuesdays, you should come next time," you lace up your sneakers and hightail it to the gym—with a smile on your face, I might add.

I confess that I have begun this cure twice and didn't make it beyond day 5 either time. It's tough to do right, and requires a certain amount of planning. Both times, though, by the second or third day, I started to run into people I hadn't seen in months on the street, in the park, on the subway—one or two people a day. It seemed like everywhere I went, there was someone I knew. Who knows what might have happened if I'd kept it up for the full nine days? If you do make it all the way through this method, be sure to let me know how it works out for you (see page 184 for contact info).

SEND HOLIDAY CARDS

If the telephone cure (previous tip) sounds like too much for you, you can apply the same basic principles to activating your social life by mail. Late November is a great time to do this, because you can use your holiday card list.

Again, you will be contacting three people a day for nine days, or one person a day for 27 days. Physically dropping a card or letter into the outgoing mail box counts as "contact" in this case. Make sure to write your letters or cards by hand, rather than on the computer, and use a red envelope. Remember to keep your message upbeat and free of complaints about anything.

Because this method is one-sided and lacks the immediacy of a conversation, it is less powerful than the telephone cure. The effort involved in following through with the telephone ritual also helps to make it more powerful. However, if your intention is strong and focused, and you use the body-speech-mind empowerment while writing and mailing your letters, this method should also help to get your social energy moving.

Feng Shui for the Personal Ads

I am a great believer in the value of personal ads for getting your dating energy moving. You might not meet the partner of your dreams through the personals, but answering and placing ads and going out on a lot of dates will help shift your energy by getting you out of the house and creating opportunities to practice your small talk. This makes it more likely that you'll meet someone you're truly interested in, although that connection may not come about through the personals.

Remember, if you only get a few call-backs from your replies to other people's ads, or if your own ad pulls in tons of responses from total losers (sorry, but this does happen), that really doesn't matter. The purpose of using the personals—just like most of the other tips in this chapter—is to engage in some kind of action that demonstrates your intention to hook up with Mr. or Ms. Right. The universe works in mysterious ways, and you might meet a cutie while you are waiting in line at the post office to buy stamps to put on all those personal ad replies.

Here are some feng shui pointers for getting the most from the personals.

CREATE A RITUAL FOR ANSWERING ADS

Make it a goal to come up with at least three sources of personal ads to answer. If you live in a major metropolitan area, you may have quite a few resources available. If you live in a smaller locale, and want to stay local, you might have fewer choices. Keep in mind that many special-interest and alumni publications have a personal ads section in the back.

The Internet now has a huge number of personals sites, including many with a specific focus that can increase your chances of meeting someone compatible. Depending on your pool of prospects, you could:

- Answer one, three, or nine ads a day for nine consecutive days

- Answer one or three ads a day for 27 consecutive days

- Answer nine ads a week for nine consecutive weeks

Cut out or print out the ads you've decided to answer. If the print ads are small, tape or glue each one to an index card. Keep your ad file in a red file folder, box or envelope in one of your Exploring or relationship power spots.

RESPONDING TO ADS BY PHONE

Make up a feng shui ritual to follow when you are answering personal ads by phone. You could:

- Wear red (feng shui power color), pink (relationships), black or dark blue (communication and connections) when it's time to make the calls

- Light a candle or some incense, and put on some romantic music to set a mood

- Take a moment to review your feng shui journal, or gaze at your "love map" collage, so what you want is firmly in your mind as you reach for the phone

- Sit in one of your romance or Exploring power spots while you make the calls

- Use the body-speech-mind empowerment method

Keep in mind that the purpose of answering an ad is to gather more information about that person. The fact that you are calling is not a promise to meet or go out. You should absolutely feel free to say, at the end of the call, something like "I appreciate your talking with me, but I have decided not to pursue this any further."

If the other person is persistent, you can end the conversation by saying something like, "I appreciate your interest, and ask that you respect my decision about what's right for me. I wish you the best of luck in connecting with someone who is a better match for you. Thanks again for your time."

You do not have to give anyone your phone number or share your last name unless you want to. If you are concerned about your number showing up on Caller ID, the easiest solution is to not call from your home phone. Look around for a reasonably private and quiet pay phone convenient to your home or office, and make your calls from there.

RESPONDING TO ADS BY MAIL

You can add feng shui oomph to your mail responses by:

- Making a short ritual around sitting down to write them (see the previous tip for ideas)

- Writing with a red pen

- Using a red envelope (this can be the envelope you will be mailing your response in, or a large red envelope for overnight empowerment)

- Ladies might use pink stationery or a pink envelope

- Placing your responses in a romance power spot overnight before mailing

- Using the body-speech-mind empowerment process before or while dropping the envelopes in the mail (focus on activating your social life and connecting up with the perfect person for you, whether or not that's the person who wrote the ad)

SENDING A PHOTO OF YOURSELF

If you are enclosing a photograph of yourself with your responses, store your photos in a red envelope or wrapped in a piece of red cloth, in a relationship power spot, until you are ready to use them. Use the body-speech-mind method to empower the photos to help connect you to your perfect partner.

MAKE UP A RITUAL FOR PLACING YOUR OWN AD

You can use the techniques for responding to ads when you place a personal ad of your own. Keep a copy of what you wrote in a red envelope. Sleep with it under your pillow for nine nights, empowering it each night to help connect you with your perfect partner. Place it in a power spot after the nine nights. When the ad is in print, cut it out, glue it to a piece of red cardboard (you can cut a piece from a red file folder), and place it in one of your relationship or Exploring power spots

FENG SHUI AND DATING SERVICES

If personal ads make you nervous, consider using a dating service. Take the paperwork this generates (your signed contract or agreement, or a receipt for your payment) and put it in a red envelope in a romance power spot, between your mattress and box spring in *kun gua* (upper right corner of bed) or sleep with it under your pillow for nine nights. Empower it to help you meet a new partner.

If you use a video service, wear something red or pink for the taping session. These colors don't have to be visible; red or pink underwear will do just fine. When you get home, place your copy of the tape in one of your romance or Exploring power spots, and use the body-speech-mind method to empower it to help you connect up with your perfect partner. If you want, you can wrap the videotape in a piece of red cloth or put it in a large red envelope.

More Feng Shui Tips for Your Social Life

POWER SPOT IMAGERY

We've already discussed how the images with which we surround ourselves exert a powerful subconscious influence on our thoughts and emotions every day. Now that you've turned your attention to meeting new people, it's important to remove any images of solitary figures from all of your relationship and Exploring power spots.

For example, back in the Centering phase you may have placed a picture of a woman in a rose garden in your sanctuary. It's a peaceful and soothing image, and appropriate for the work of that stage.

Now that you have moved into the Exploring phase, however, you'll want to find another place for that image, because it shows a woman alone, and you are now focused on meeting your next partner. Replace it with an image that shows a couple in a romantic environment.

As you go around your home, you may be surprised by how many images of solitary figures you find—this is common in the homes of people who complain of being single, and is easy to fix.

SPREAD THE WORD

We've been focusing in the Exploring phase on activating WATER energy and *kan gua*, but let's not forget about *li gua*, which governs your fame and reputation. Dig out your floor plan again, and look for where *li gua* is in your home, bedroom, and living room. Is there an opportunity in any of those places for you to hang a large mirror? If there is, empower the mirror to enhance your reputation and image—how you are seen by others. You can also hang a bell or wind chime in *li gua* and empower it to "spread the word" that you are available and to call your next partner to you.

INTRODUCE YOURSELF

Here's a deceptively simple way to activate your social life: introduce yourself to at least one new person a day for nine days. If you're feeling ambitious, keep it up for 27 days. You must exchange names and telephone numbers for the introduction to count.

This is not difficult to do if you are a sales professional, attend a lot of conferences and trade shows, or love to go bar- or club-hopping. If you are naturally shy and don't normally interact with many people each day, it can be quite a challenge—which means it will be very powerful for you!

THE HAIR-DO CURE

This is my all-time favorite silly feng shui cure for meeting new people. What you do is wear your hair in a different style every three days for fifteen days. In other words, wear your hair one way for three days, then another way for three days, and so on. (Yes, you may shampoo daily; just redo your hair in the same or a different style, as appropriate.)

Gamines with pixie-cuts will have a tough time with this one, but if your hair is shoulder-length or longer it's quite doable, and rather fun. When was the last time you wore your hair in Pocahontas braids, or up in a bun, or just parted on the other side? A new cut or color counts as a change, too. It's all about breaking out of your appearance rut. I do recommend looking ahead in your calendar for upcoming special events, and doing a little advance planning, so you don't show up at a stuffy business meeting in pigtails.

I learned this as a method for women to use, but there's no reason guys couldn't do it, too, if their hair is long enough and they are willing to be creative. Remember to use the body-speech-mind empowerment while you're fixing your hair every morning.

ACTIVATE YOUR CAR

You spend a lot of time in your car, so why not include it in your feng shui strategy? One thing you can do is hang a pink faceted crystal ball from the rearview mirror with a 9" or 18" piece of red string, ribbon, or cord. (Hang it at a height that's convenient, then tie up the extra string in a bow.) Empower it to attract romance to you everywhere you go.

If you find the dancing rainbows created by the crystal distracting while you are driving, you could hang a cupid figure or two red hearts from the rearview mirror instead.

KEEP AN OPEN MIND

Take advantage of *every* opportunity to mingle and be sociable, even if you think it will be a waste of time.

I met one boyfriend this way. I had been invited to a party that I had no interest in going to, and where I was sure I would meet no one compatible. But I knew I couldn't ask the universe to hook me up without "walking the talk," so staying home was not an option. I went, and a party game paired us up—otherwise we might have been in the same room all evening without speaking to each other. Don't make assumptions about what is or is not a good place to meet someone! You really never know.

This isn't so much a feng shui cure as much as it is good social-life advice. You can, however, use feng shui techniques—such as keeping invitations in an Exploring power spot, and using the body-speech-mind empowerment before you go out the door—to make everything you do just that little bit more effective.

Expand Your Horizons

One good way to create a shift in your energy is to do something new or different every day. This doesn't have to be anything major, so long as you consciously create variations in your daily routine.

When you follow the same routines day after day, it's easy to slip into sleep-walking mode. Connecting up with someone new requires that you be alert and open to all possibilities, which means you need to stay awake and be in the moment.

TRY SOMETHING NEW

Take a yoga or qigong class. Sign up for a writing or gardening workshop. Volunteer your time to a local charitable organization. Climb a mountain. See if you still remember how to ride a bike. Do something that tourists do when they visit your town. Or you could:

- Listen to a different radio station or talk show
- Read a magazine or book on a new topic
- Wear something completely different, just for the hell of it
- Eat something different, or go to a new restaurant
- Take a different route to or home from work
- Go for a walk or a drive in a different neighborhood
- Stop at a different coffee shop for breakfast

Participate fully in whatever you decide to do, and hold your intention to welcome new experiences and people into your life firmly in your heart and mind.

Moving On

You'll know when you're moving out of the Exploring stage of the Relationship Cycle when you meet someone you really "click" with and you start going out with that person regularly.

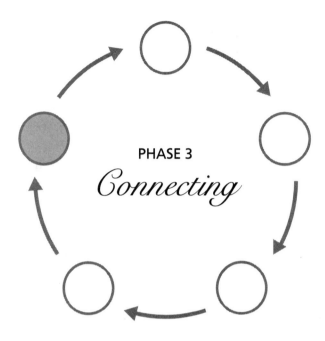

PHASE 3

Connecting

The third stage in your journey through the Relationship Cycle is Connecting. There's still progress to be made, but you no longer feel alone, because you've met someone with whom you imagine having a committed, long-term relationship.

Your most important task for the Connecting stage of the cycle is to turn your home into a space that welcomes and nourishes romance. You've already started this work with the space clearing and clutter-clearing efforts of the past two phases, and with the attention you've given to your front door and entryway.

Now that you've met someone whom you are beginning to date seriously, it's time to turn your focus to *kun gua* (relationships) and your bedroom. Before we get into details, let's take a few minutes to explore the broader context of Connecting and how it relates to the feng shui energy system.

The Wood Element in Feng Shui

The Connecting phase is associated with the WOOD element in feng shui. We can gain a greater understanding of the qualities and objectives of this stage by exploring the meanings and characteristics of wood.

In feng shui, the WOOD element is associated both with early spring, when the first green shoots push up through the bare earth, and with early summer when plants have grown tall and green and lush. The movement of WOOD is expansive and uplifting—the energy of easy growth and development. The colors associated with WOOD are all shades of green.

In Traditional Chinese Medicine, WOOD is associated with the liver and gall bladder. The emotion affected by WOOD imbalance is anger. As we move into the Connecting stage of the Relationship Cycle and start to form a romantic attachment with a new partner, we are vulnerable to any unresolved anger from past relationships surfacing again in a new context.

The sound associated with WOOD is "shouting," which you may find yourself doing if there are any tensions brewing in your new relationship. This is an important time to pay close attention to any patterns from past relationships that may be recurring now. These are an indication to explore your reasons for being attracted to this specific person. Are you repeating a pattern of falling for a particular type of person who for one reason or another is unable to give you the love, attention, and respect that you deserve? Or perhaps you are saying and doing things in this new relationship that are driven more by your experiences with past partners than by what is actually taking place this time.

The "virtue" of WOOD is kindness. When this energy is strong you are able to listen and respond to others with objectivity, and to be comfortable when other's opinions do not dovetail neatly with your point of view. When the WOOD element is too strong, you may become stubborn and opinionated, unable or unwilling to listen to perspectives other than your own.

When WOOD energy is weak, you may lose your "spine." You get along easily with others, but without contributing any insight or personal opinion.

JOURNALING

Find some quiet time to explore your personal experience of the WOOD relationship phase. Think about how you have reacted to the challenges and opportunities of Connecting as you moved through this phase in the past.

- How do you usually respond to this phase, both emotionally and physically?

- What aspects of nurturing and supporting a new relationship are easy for you? Which are difficult?

- What do you most look forward to about this stage?

- What specific situations or behaviors in the context of a relationship tend to make you angry? What can you learn from that, and how can you avoid that this time around?

Think about what personal challenges are likely to surface for you in this phase of the relationship cycle. This might include:

- Getting so carried away by the excitement of a new relation-ship that you forget to keep an eye on what you need to receive from a partner in order to be happy in the long run

- Being aware of any tendency to withhold or suppress your real wants or feelings in order to be more lovable

Wood Energy and the Ba Gua

The WOOD element is associated with *jen* (family) and *hsun* (wealth) *guas*. *Jen* is located at the center of the left side of the *ba gua*,* with *hsun gua* above it in the far left corner.

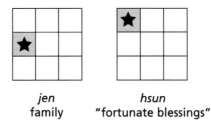

jen
family

hsun
"fortunate blessings"

If you are placing the *ba gua* according to the compass, *jen gua* is in the east, and *hsun gua* is in the south east.

From the perspective of the Connecting phase of the Relationship Cycle, *jen* and *hsun guas* have to do with new beginnings, the growth of a new relationship, and with exploring the "fortunate blessings" that you each have to offer the other.

WOOD is nourished by WATER, so all kinds of water features and plants are great additions to your home now. FIRE energy will burn up WOOD, so stick with green and pink as your relationship power colors now, and avoid bringing too many red items into the house. Remember, too, that METAL will chop up WOOD, unless there's lots of WATER around to create a three-element arc of the creative cycle.

---

* Did I just hear you say, "Uh, excuse me, but you missed one"? Moving clockwise around the *ba gua* from *kan* to *jen guas*, we have jumped over *ken gua* (self-understanding), because it is associated with EARTH, and in Phase 3: Connecting, we are focusing on the WOOD element. We'll take a closer look at *ken gua* when we get to Phase 5 of the Relationship Cycle.

YOUR CONNECTING BA GUA

Once again, you can draw an empty *ba gua* grid on a sheet of paper or photocopy the *ba gua* template on page 204. Write "Connecting" in the middle (*tai chi*) square.

Start with *jen gua*—the middle of the left side. Write in "family" and any other specific meaning this area may have for you, based on your personal issues and goals for the Connecting phase. In *hsun gua*—the back left corner—note what "fortunate blessings" means to you in the context of a new relationship.

Now, think about the other *guas* (there's a *ba gua* map on page 188 if you need to look these up), and identify any personal meanings they may have for you in the Connecting stage. Remember that there are no right or wrong answers; this is your *ba gua*, based on your feelings, and it's okay to leave some areas blank.

You may have come up with something like this:

will he give me what I want, need from a partner?		am I ready to get more involved?
family issues	CONNECTING	does he want kids?
compatible spiritual beliefs	open, honest communication	

Find Your Connecting Power Spots

Once again we're going to fine-tune your power spots. This time you'll want to compare the location of your relationship power spots with the key *guas* that you've decided deserve attention during the Connecting phase.

First, look to see if *jen* or *hsun guas* of your home, bedroom, personal sanctuary* or other key room overlap with any of your relationship power spots.

If you are placing the *ba gua* according to the entry, also take a look at the compass directions. Are any of your relationship power spots in the east or southeastern sectors of your home or of that room?

You may find several areas of overlap, or none. If you don't find any areas of overlap, focus your feng shui efforts on *kun gua* and your bedroom, and then apply the guidelines in this chapter to other power spots throughout the house. As we go along, you'll learn lots of ways to turn your home and bedroom into spaces that attract and nurture a blossoming relationship.

As always, pay attention to your intuition as you choose which changes to make to your home. Use your Connecting *ba gua* to help you fine-tune your affirmations and visualizations during this phase. As you focus on the needs of your new relationship, remember to reserve some quiet time for yourself every day so you can stay in touch with your feelings, and to record your insights in your feng shui journal.

---

*   See pages 88-92 in the Centering chapter.

Feng Shui for the Connecting Phase

How to Correct a Missing Kun Gua

When *kun gua*, the area associated with romance, is missing from your floor plan, it can affect the stability of existing relationships and make it more difficult for a single person to connect with a new partner. When we place the *ba gua* according to the front door, *kun gua* is always in the far right corner of the house. You may also wish to check your home layout for any missing area in the southwest area of the home, as that is the compass direction associated with *kun*.

If you are not sure whether or not you have a "missing" *kun gua*, turn to pages 190-191 in the Appendix for guidance. If you know you have a missing *kun gua*, here are some things you can—and should—do to enhance this very important area of your home.

EXTERIOR CURES

Place a light, flag pole, tiki torch, large stone, statue, or tree in the exact spot where the corner of the building would be if the area were not missing. You can also use a floral border, hedge, or fence to define where the walls would be if the area were not missing. A bird feeder will activate that spot by attracting the living energy of birds (and squirrels!), and a bird bath could also be used if you live in a climate where it will be in use all year round. I don't recommend a bird bath if it will be frozen or empty for months at a time.

Whatever cure you choose, make sure that your placement is very accurate. Just a few inches out of alignment will make a difference to the effectiveness of the cure.

If you already have a porch, deck, balcony, or patio that takes up that space, here are some ways to activate it:

• Place a light or plant at the outside corner

• Place a row of plants along the railing

• Wrap a strand of lights or flags around the railing

• Plant a hedge to border the patio

Kun gua is associated with the EARTH element. EARTH is created by FIRE*, so any kind of light cure is appropriate here.

Plants are among my favorite feng shui solutions, because they bring living beauty to the area you are working on. Do be aware, however, that plants are associated with the WOOD element, which uproots EARTH. When you use plants as a cure in *kun gua*, it's a good idea to also add some FIRE energy to that area. This could be as simple as choosing plants with red blossoms, placing the plant in a red pot, or even tying a red ribbon around the pot.

You should also add a touch of the FIRE element if you use a METAL cure in *kun gua*, because METAL will reduce the strength of EARTH. Pointed or triangular shapes can also be used to represent the FIRE element, if you don't want to use red.

INTERIOR MIRROR CURES

Those of you who live in an apartment and can't use an exterior cure will be glad to know that there are a variety of things you can do from the inside.

---

*   If you need to refresh your understanding of the Creative, Controlling and Reducing cycles of the Elements, you can turn to pages 198-201.

You can correct a missing *kun gua* by placing a large mirror on an interior wall so that the reflection implies a virtual room where there is none. You can even place two mirrors, one on each inside wall of the missing area, if you want to. For even better effect, place something with symbolic imagery related to your goals where the mirror will reflect it into the *kun gua* space:

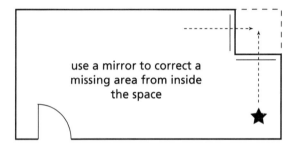

If you can't place a mirror in the appropriate spot because there is a window in that section of the wall, you can hang a mirror on the opposite wall, where it will reflect the window (and the view through the window). Empower the mirror to connect the outside energy in the *kun* area with the interior of the house.

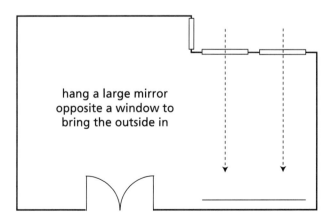

OTHER THINGS YOU CAN DO

If using a mirror is not appropriate, or you don't like the way it looks, you can bring *kun gua* back into balance by strengthening *kun gua* in your bedroom and living room, as well as any other relationship power spots in your home.

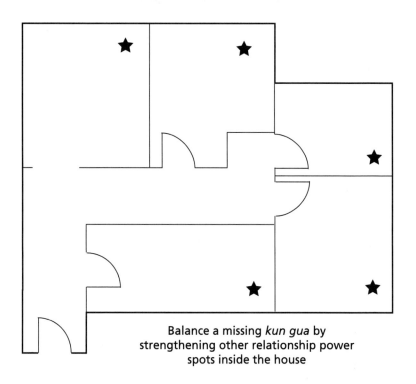

Balance a missing *kun gua* by
strengthening other relationship power
spots inside the house

EMPOWER YOUR CHANGES

Whatever you choose to do to correct a missing *kun gua*, be sure to use the body-speech-mind empowerment method (pages 10-12). Visualize the *chi* of *kun gua* becoming full and strong, to support and illuminate your new relationship.

Attract Chi to Your Power Spots

Now that you've worked on your entry in order to enhance your social-connections (Phase 2), let's figure out how to get more of that energy to your bedroom and other relationship power spots.

CLEAR A PATH TO YOUR BEDROOM

With floor plan in hand, start at your front door, and physically walk the most direct route to your bedroom. You can use a colored pencil to draw the path on your floor plan.

Remember that feng shui means "wind and water" and that *chi* likes to flow through your home like a gentle breeze or a meandering stream. As you walk from the front door to your bedroom, imagine that you are a current of nourishing *chi*. Pay attention to any places where your path is blocked or your direction diverted by clutter, furniture, or the layout of your home.

Repeat this exercise for your other relationship power spots, and make a note on your floor plan of any improvements you can make—such as rearranging furniture, keeping certain doors open or closed, or placing important imagery at key focal points—that will help encourage the flow of *chi* to these important power spots.

ATTRACT CHI TO YOUR POWER SPOTS

If your bedroom or other major relationship power spot is a long way from the front door, hang a bell or wind chime in that spot, or in the doorway to that room, and empower it to attract more *chi* there. You can also enhance the *chi* of that spot by cleaning the windows to let more light in, or by adding brighter lights.

USE PLANTS TO ATTRACT CHI TO YOUR BEDROOM

Another good way to attract *chi* to a bedroom that is a long way from the front door is with potted houseplants. Standing at your front door, look toward the bedroom. Find the spot where your line of vision ends, and place a lush green plant there. Now, move to that spot, look toward the bedroom again, and place another plant at the next point where the path to the bedroom continues out of your line of sight.

Continue placing plants as "signposts" along the way until you are at the bedroom, then place one more plant inside the bedrooom where it will be seen from the doorway (if that spot can be in *kun gua* in the bedroom, that's even better).

Ideally, you should use three, six, or nine plants (remember that multiples of three are feng shui power numbers) for this. I recommend using the same kind of plant, if you can. You may also be glad to know that you do not have to use real plants for this cure—life-like artificial plants will do. If you are not good with houseplants, or the positions you have identified for placing plants will not provide natural light, artificial plants will probably be a better choice for you.

CREATE A PATH WITH FLOWERS

If you love fresh, fragrant flowers as much as I do, you could do the preceding plants cure with blossoming plants, or even with bouquets of fresh flowers. Chose red, pink and white blossoms, as those are the feng shui colors associated with *kun gua* and romance.

Using fresh flowers or blossoming plants is more ambitious, since you will need to keep a watchful eye on the freshness of the blossoms. If orchids are within budgetary reach, they would be a good choice because the blooms last for such a long time.

Once again, life-like artificial plants are an acceptable substitute. Use the body-speech-mind method to empower your life-like plants and flowers to direct *chi* as strongly as living plants do.

OPEN YOUR BEDROOM DOOR

Your entire bedroom is always an important relationship power spot, so make sure this room's "mouth of *chi*" is clear and unobstructed as well.

The door should open all the way without hitting any pieces of furniture, and should not have anything stowed behind it. If it suits your style, you may want to hang a cupid or cherub image either on or above the bedroom door, to welcome romantic *chi* into your private space.

If you are in the habit of keeping your bedroom door closed most of the time—even when you are not at home or not in the bedroom—try leaving it open except when you need privacy. When you shut the door, you block the flow of *chi* into the bedroom; if your bedroom door is closed for most of the hours of the day, it could be contributing to a lack of fresh air in your love life.

Create an Environment for Romance

I've mentioned before that your bedroom is your most important relationship power spot, because it is the space most strongly imbued with your wishes, dreams, aspirations, and personal *chi*. While good feng shui throughout your house will help create a stage for more positive experiences, when it comes to romance your bedroom receives the focus of our attention.

Here are some ways you can ensure that your bedroom has strong romance *chi* and that it will support and nourish your new relationship.

FIRST IMPRESSIONS

In feng shui, as in the rest of life, first impressions count for a lot, so make sure your bedroom makes a good one.

Your bedroom is such a familiar place to you, you may no longer notice what it really looks like, especially to a first-time visitor. Try this: wherever you are right now, close your eyes and imagine you are standing in your bedroom doorway. What do you see? What catches your attention first?

Now think about what's in *kun gua* in your bedroom (standing in the doorway, *kun gua* will be the far right corner of the room.

If you are in your bedroom, step out into the hallway and close the door behind you. If you are not in your bedroom, go there and (staying out in the hall and trying not to look inside) close the bedroom door.

Face the bedroom door, close your eyes, and take a few deep breaths to get clear and centered.

Reach out (with eyes still closed) and push the door open.

Now open your eyes.

- What is the first thing you see?

- What did you notice next?

- What most catches your attention?

- Did you experience a body shift when you first looked into your bedroom? Did you tense up, or did you relax?

- Did what you see make you smile, or did it put a grimace on your face?

- If your dream date rang the doorbell right now, would your bedroom pass inspection?

- What does your bedroom say about you to a first-time visitor?

Here are some pointers for buffing up that all-important first impression, depending on what you first see when entering the bedroom:

A blank wall
If the first thing you see when entering your bedroom is a blank wall, you can improve the *chi* of the room by:

- Hanging a romantic image there

- Placing a vase of beautiful fresh flowers, or a romantic object or image of some kind on a table or dresser placed opposite the doorway

A wall less than six feet in front of you
If the first thing you see when entering your bedroom is a wall directly in front of you, you can improve the *chi* of the room by hanging a mirror there to open up the space (see page 116 for details on a blocked entry).

Artwork

If the first thing you see when entering your bedroom is a piece of artwork, you can improve the *chi* of the room by making sure it is an attractive and romantic image.

Table or dresser

If the first thing you see when entering your bedroom is a table or dresser, you can improve the *chi* of the room by:

- Making sure it is dusted, polished, tidy, and in good repair
- Placing a lamp, vase of flowers, or romantic object on it

Bookcase

If the first thing you see when entering your bedroom is a bookcase, you can improve the *chi* of the room by:

- Taking every single book or other item off the shelves, dusting them, and dusting/polishing the shelves
- Reshelving everything neatly
- Leaving room on the shelves (aim for 25%) open for new things

A couch or chair

If the first thing you see when entering your bedroom is a couch or chair, you can improve the *chi* of the room by:

- Covering worn upholstery with a pretty slip-cover
- Putting away any clothes or other belongings piled on the seat
- Removing all pet hair from the upholstery
- Replacing a single seat with seating for two (a love seat or pair of chairs)

Your desk

If the first thing you see when entering your bedroom is your desk, you can improve the *chi* of the room by relocating your work space to a more appropriate area.

A window

If the first thing you see when entering your bedroom is a window, you can improve the *chi* of the room by:

- Hanging sheer curtains to obscure a less-than gorgeous view

- Hanging a faceted crystal ball in front of the window to keep *chi* from leaking out

Closet door

If the first thing you see when entering your bedroom is a closet door, you can improve the *chi* of the room by:

- Cleaning out the closet

- Getting rid of things you no longer need or want

- Leaving closet space available (aim for 25%) for your next partner's things

- Keeping the closet door closed

- Hanging a curtain in front of a closet that does not have a door

Your bed

If the first thing you see when entering your bedroom is your bed, you can improve the *chi* of the room by making up the bed before you leave the house in the morning, so it is neat and tidy when you come home. Pink or green sheets, coverlet, or throw pillows create a romantic, welcoming impression.

MIRRORS IN THE BEDROOM

Round and oval mirrors are auspicious in the bedroom because the circular shape implies completion and unity. Hang one in *kun gua* of the bedroom, or on the wall above the head of your bed, and empower it to expand your relationship *chi*. Make sure that anything you hang above the head of the bed is securely fastened to the wall; concern that your feng shui cures might fall on you in the middle of the night will undermine their effectiveness!

CREATE A SPACE TO BE TOGETHER

Make sure that at least one of your relationship power spots includes a sitting area where the two of you can spend time relaxing together. A pair of comfy chairs in a quiet corner is good; a loveseat is even better.

ACTIVATE THE TAI CHI

The *tai chi* is the area at the center of the *ba gua*. Because it connects all eight of the outer *guas*, whatever is going on energetically in the *tai chi* of your home will affect all the *guas*.

Check the *tai chi* area of your home to make sure it is clean and free of clutter, then activate it to support a happy love life. Appropriate ways to activate the *tai chi* include:

- A large faceted crystal ball (since you are activating romance, a pink crystal is appropriate, or use a clear one)

- A plant with red, pink, or white blossoms

- A piece of artwork or statuary with a romantic theme

- The *tai chi* symbol (*yin-yang*), which represents the interconnected, ever-changing, eternal balance of the male (*yang*) and female (*yin*) qualities of *chi*

Romantic Imagery and Symbols

The Connecting phase of the Relationship Cycle is a good time to enhance your relationship power spots with romantic imagery and symbols. The *tai chi* symbol shown on the previous page is just one of the traditional images that can be effective in enhancing *kun gua* and other relationship power spots. Other options are provided here, followed by some western alternatives.

CHINESE SYMBOLS OF LOVE AND FIDELITY

These Chinese symbols of love and fidelity, traditionally associated with marriage, can be used in *kun gua* or anywhere you'd like to enhance relationship *chi*:

- A pair of mandarin ducks

- A pair of butterflies

- The double-happiness symbol

- Peach blossoms are associated with the growth of new love, but are short-lived and the romance may be, too; if you use peach blossom imagery, add a symbol of fidelity as well

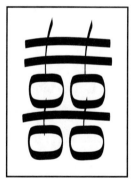

double happiness

OTHER ROMANTIC IMAGERY

Art reproductions or photographs of lovers courting, embracing, or kissing are always good for *kun gua*. And of course all the traditional symbols of romance—hearts, flowers, roses, cupids, valentines—are good to use in your power spots.

You can use cherub and angel pictures or figures as feng shui cures for romance, too; place them in a romance power spot and empower them to bring you luck in your new relationship.

Look in museum store catalogs and poster shops for romantic imagery that appeals to you and that will suit the style and decor of your home. Invest in an inexpensive frame, and hang in your bedroom or other romance power spot.

TWO IS YOUR LUCKY NUMBER

Pairs of anything imply partnership; look in your relationship power spots for opportunities to group pairs of objects together, such as:

- Two red roses in a vase
- Two candles or candlesticks
- Two heart-shaped throw pillows on your loveseat
- A picture or figurine of swans, doves, or other birds in pairs

THINK PINK

Pink is the color of romance, and *kun gua* loves it! Use it for home accessories for your bedroom and relationship power spots:

- Sleep on pink sheets
- Paint your bedroom pink
- Buy three or nine sets of new pink underwear, so you can wear pink intimately every day for 27 days (yes, of course you can wash your undies between wearings)

GREEN IS GOOD, TOO

Can't stand pink, or it's just too girly for you? You'll be glad to hear that green is an acceptable alternative. Choose the lighter, more spring-like and pastel shades of green, and empower it to help your new relationship blossom and grow like flowers in the spring.

Moving on...

Your transition through the Connecting phase might be gradual or it may flash past practically overnight. You and your new beau may want to take your time getting to know each other before you decide to date each other exclusively. At the other extreme, you may connect with someone and barely have time to buy new pink sheets for your bed before you realize you are madly and mutually in love. The Loving stage begins when you both consider yourselves a couple, are no longer casual about the relationship, and are no longer seeing other people at the same time.

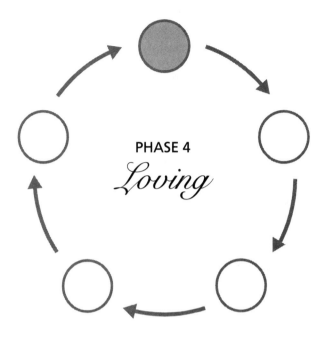

PHASE 4

Loving

The fourth stage in your journey through the Relationship Cycle is Loving. My work as your feng shui relationship coach is almost done; while a life-long commitment has not yet been made, as one half of a loving couple you are not really single any more.

Our focus in the Loving stage is on removing potential causes of disharmony and conflict from your bedroom and from the rest of your home in order to encourage open communication and to support your stability and future as a couple.

All of the work that you have done to clean, rearrange, and beautify your home has created a good foundation for the work of the Loving phase. Before we begin, let's take a closer look at the qualities and characteristics of this stage from the perspective of feng shui.

The Fire Element in Feng Shui

The Loving phase of the Relationship Cycle is associated with the FIRE element in feng shui. What comes to mind when you think about fire?

Fire can be exciting or threatening. It can warm us in winter, or rage out of control and burn down a house or threaten an entire forest. We see FIRE energy in the romantic flame of a candle and feel it in the pounding of our heart when we are passionately in love.

In feng shui, FIRE is associated with the heat and intensity of mid-summer when the sun is high and hot in the sky. FIRE is active and expansive, and its colors are red and orange.

In Traditional Chinese Medicine, FIRE is associated with the heart; its sound is "laughing." This is often the most joyful and exhilarating stage of romance, and we float through life with a smile for everyone.

An imbalance in the FIRE energy associated with being in love can lead to overexcitement and a lack of perspective. When you are in the Loving phase of the Relationship Cycle it is easy to have "stars in your eyes" and become "blinded by love."

The "virtues" of FIRE are compassion and respect for others. When this energy is healthy you interact appropriately with others and are able to express your emotions effectively. When the FIRE element is too strong, you may become arrogant and self-centered, oblivious to the wants and needs of others. When FIRE *chi* is weak, you may appear callous or hard-hearted due to your inability to express the feelings you have deep inside.

JOURNALING

Find some quiet time to reflect on your personal experience of the FIRE phase in past relationships. Think about how you've reacted to the challenges and opportunities of Loving as you moved through this phase in the past.

- How do you usually respond to this phase, both emotionally and physically?

- What aspects of experiencing and expressing the full heart that comes with Loving are easy for you? Which are difficult?

- What aspects of being in love do you tend to overdo? Does the intensity of love distort your perspective?

- Do you fall in love too easily, racing ahead of your partner emotionally, so the two of you become out of sync? Or do you tend to hold back as your partner moves forward?

- What insight, if any, have you gained from exploring FIRE energy from a feng shui perspective?

Think about what personal challenges are likely to surface for you in this phase of the relationship cycle. This may include being sensitive to the feelings of your single friends; sure, they're happy for you, but try not to talk about how wonderful your new lover is *all* the time.

Fire Energy and the Ba Gua

The FIRE element is associated with *li gua* (fame and reputation) at the center of the far side of the *ba gua*, opposite *kan gua*:

li
fame & reputation

If you are placing the *ba gua* according to the compass directions, *li gua* is in the south.

From the perspective of the Loving phase of the Relationship Cycle, *li gua* has to do with establishing who you are as a couple, both with each other and in the eyes of the world.

FIRE is nourished by WOOD, so all the plants and flowers you brought into the house in the Connecting phase will continue to support you now. WATER extinquishes FIRE, so if you have placed an indoor fountain in a relationship power spot, be sure to arrange some houseplants around it, to create a WATER-WOOD-FIRE arc of the Creative Cycle.

Check your *li gua* power spots to make sure there isn't too much EARTH energy there. EARTH depletes FIRE's energy, unless there is WOOD around to support FIRE.

Find Your Loving Power Spots

Once again we're going to explore the different areas of the *ba gua*, this time from the perspective of the Loving phase. Draw a nine-square grid, or photocopy page 204, and write "Loving" in the middle (*tai chi*) square.

Start with *li gua*—the square in the center of the top row. Write in "how we are seen as a couple" and any other specific meaning this area may have for you, based on your personal issues and goals for the Loving phase.

Now, think about the other *guas* (there's a *ba gua* map on page 188 if you need to look them up), and identify any personal meanings they may have for you in the Loving stage. You might come up with something like this:

celebrate our good fortune!	how are we seen as a couple?	keep it strong!
meeting his parents & ex-wife!	LOVING	will his kids accept me?
	find work in LA?	move to LA to be with him?

To find your power spots for the Loving phase, compare the location of your relationship power spots with any key *guas* that you've decided deserve some attention now.

First, look to see if *li gua* of your home, bedroom, sanctuary or other key room overlaps with any of your relationship power spots. If you have placed the *ba gua* according to the entry, also take a look at the compass directions. Are any of your relationship power spots in the southern sectors of your home or of that room?

You may find several overlap areas, or none. If you don't find any areas of overlap, focus your feng shui efforts on *kun gua* and your bedroom, and then apply the guidelines in this chapter to other power spots throughout the house. As we go along, you'll learn lots of ways to ensure that your home and bedroom are spaces that will support a stable and lasting relationship. Remember to use your Loving *ba gua* to help you fine-tune your affirmations and visualizations during this phase.

Feng Shui for the Loving Phase

The previous chapters have focused on attracting a new romantic relationship into your life. Now that you have found someone, it's a good time to reevaluate the *chi* of your bedroom to make sure it supports a stable and long-lasting relationship.

This is also a good time to go around your home—especially your bedroom—and remove any cures that you put into place while you were looking to meet someone new. Now that you are with someone, any "I'm still looking" energy you leave in place could undermine the stability of your new relationship.

I don't mean that you need to undo *all* the changes you've made in the previous phases—although there may be some that should go. If you are no longer answering personal ads, for example, clear those red power envelopes and personals from your relationship power spots. Other changes that you've made, such as opening up the area around your front door, can now be re-empowered with the body-speech-mind method to bring success and happiness in your new relationship into the home.

Because imagery is so important in feng shui, this would be a good time to put a photograph of the two of you in a beautiful frame, and display it prominently in *li gua*. This will facilitate your shift from being two separate individuals to being recognized and thought of as a couple—by each other and by everyone who knows and meets you.

Balance and Harmony in the Bedroom

As you review this section, keep in mind that in many cases you will not be able to achieve the ideal arrangement of your furniture, because following one guideline may contradict another. Placing your bed in the command position, for example, may put it in front of a window. Recognize that your goal is to make the best use of your space, whatever it's limitations may be. Use your knowledge of feng shui and your intuition to guide your decisions.

COMMAND POSITION

It is just as important for your bed to be in the command position now that you are a couple as it was when you were single. (If you don't know what the command position is, take a moment now to read pages 83-84 in Phase 1.)

EQUAL OPPORTUNITY SPACE

In addition to using the command position, you should also try to position the bed so there is equal space on either side of it. If one side of the bed is against or close to the wall, the person who sleeps on that side will be disempowered in the relationship and over time may start to feel emotionally trapped. The person on the more open side of the bed, on the other hand, will have greater freedom of movement, and this can potentially lead to that person leaving the relationship.

NIGHTSTANDS AND BEDSIDE LAMPS

Each side of the bed should have its own nightstand and reading lamp, to avoid any imbalance in energy that could cause instability in the relationship. They don't have to match, but should be of similar size and wattage.

HEADBOARDS

A sturdy bed supports a stable relationship. In feng shui terms, a headboard provides protection and security—but only if securely attached to the bed frame, and ideally to the wall as well.

If you don't have a headboard, consider getting one. Solid wood or upholstered headboards are considered better (in feng shui terms) than slatted wood or iron bars.

Headboards with built-in shelves are frowned on in feng shui, because the edges of the shelves can send disruptive energy at you while you sleep. Covering the shelves with fabric at night is an easy solution.

If you can't afford a headboard, you can:

- Use paint, wallpaper, or fabric to decorate the section of wall behind the head of the bed, and empower it to act as a headboard.

- Place a symbol of protection on the wall over the head of the bed. This could be an animal figure such as a dragon or tiger that you empower to protect you, or a guardian spirit or deity of any kind.

SPACE BEHIND THE BED

If your bed is in the corner, angled into the room, you may be in a great command position, but the triangular space behind the head of the bed will be a source of unstable energy. In this position, a headboard is considered essential. Place a light or plant in the space behind the bed, and empower it to stabilize the energy there.

A bed that is placed in front of a window is also in a weak feng shui position. If you cannot avoid this placement, hang a faceted crystal ball in the window or over the head of the bed. Remember to use a red string cut to a multiple of nine inches to hang your crystal, and empower it to provide stability and protection.

KING SIZE BED

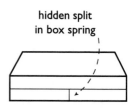

The box spring for a king size bed is really two box springs side by side, with a king mattress on top of them. This creates a division between the two sides of the bed, which can create a division in the relationship.

To cure this, you will need a red fitted sheet or about three yards of red fabric. Red is the feng shui power color; it seals the energetic split between the box springs to create a solid foundation for the relationship.

Remove the mattress and place the fitted sheet or fabric over the division in the box springs, making sure it completely covers the split on the top and sides. Tuck the ends underneath. You may need help with this (king mattresses are heavy!); ask your partner to lend a hand, so you can both put your energy into the cure.

OVERHEAD BEAMS

Exposed ceiling beams create pressure on the area directly beneath them. A beam over your bed can do more than just prevent you from sleeping well; if the beam runs runs lengthwise over the bed it is likely to have a negative effect on the relationship.

- A beam over the middle of the bed causes a division between the partners. The couple may have trouble communicating, make love less often, or even split up.

- A beam over one side of the bed will affect one person but not the other, creating imbalance in the relationship.

The lower the ceiling, the greater the impact of an overhead beam will be. If you are in a high-ceilinged room, and are suffering no ill consequences, don't fret about it. Keep in mind as well the importance of having the bed in the command position; you may have to choose one or the other, and may need to try both for a while to see which position is best for you.

If you can't avoid an exposed beam over your bed, you can lessen the impact by placing something under either end of the beam that will symbolically lift it up.

• Bamboo flutes (you'll need two) are the traditional solution. You can hang one flute vertically on the wall under either each end of the beam, so that the natural growth direction of the wood points up (usually this is with the mouthpiece at the top).

Another option is to hang the two flutes on the side of the beam. Here the flutes should be at a 45-degree angle, so they create the shape of the top of an octagon, thus implying the octagonal shape of the traditional *ba gua*.

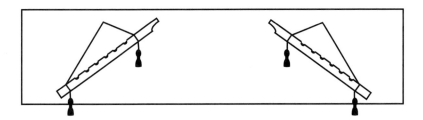

Hang the flutes with red string cut to a multiple of nine inches, and add a red tassel or two to each flute if they didn't come with any.

• If flutes don't appeal to you, use plants or uplights.

• Use imagery under the ends of the beam, or along the side of the beam, to symbolically lift the energy. Appropriate images include angels, birds in flight, and the like.

• Disguise the beam with fabric or a canopy over the bed

- Hang a vine, garland, or string of miniature lights along the side or bottom of the beam

- Hang three faceted crystal balls (with red string cut to a multiple of nine inches) from the underside of the beam: one at each end and one in the middle.

CEILING FANS

A ceiling fan over your bed may keep you cool and comfy on hot nights (that's a plus), but it is also creating a swirl of "cutting" *chi* from the blades spinning around (that's not good). Replace the pull-chain with a faceted crystal ball on red string, and empower it to deflect any cutting *chi* from reaching the bed.

SLANTED CEILINGS

Chi flows down the slope of a slanted ceiling and puts pressure on whatever is against the lower wall. If your bed is on the low side of a room with a slanted ceiling, you will be under a lot of pressure while you sleep. The height of the ceiling, the angle of slope, and the size of the room affect how much pressure is created. If you cannot stand up on the low side of the room without bumping your head, the situation is considered severe.

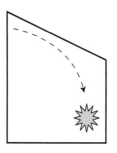

Even in a high-ceilinged bedroom, the lopsided nature of the space will create unbalanced energy in the relationship. One or both of you may feel stressed-out, off-balance, irritable, moody, or out-of-sorts much of the time, and you each may start to think of your partner as unstable or unreliable. Yikes! Time for feng shui help. Here are some things you can do:

- Put a canopy over your bed, or hang a swag of fabric above the bed to disguise the uneven height of the ceiling
- Place three uplights along the shorter wall to lift *chi* on that side of the room
- Hang a faceted crystal ball over a bed on the lower side of the room, and empower it to protect you

You may be glad to know that a cathedral ceiling, which slopes down symmetrically on either side of a high center line, is less of a concern, because the energy of the room is more evenly balanced. Nevertheless, you may want to think twice about how you arrange your furniture in the space, in order to minimize the effect of the increased pressure along the sides of the room. A ceiling with a flat center portion and angled sides is usually not a problem.

ANGLED WALLS

When two walls meet at anything other than a 90-degree angle, the *chi* in that space will be affected. An accute angle creates pressure, and a wide angle can accelerate and destabilize *chi*. Neither effect is a good thing. Hang the image of a protective figure or deity on the angled wall and empower it to shield you from any negative influence.

"SEEING RED" IS A GOOD THING

Red is the feng shui power color, associated with luck, success, and the energy of FIRE. If your new relationship is moving too slowly to suit you, put a lamp with a red light-bulb in *kun gua*, and sleep on red sheets. Drape a string of novelty lights shaped like red-hot chili peppers in a *kun gua* power spot to spice up your love life!

THREE THINGS TO REMOVE FROM YOUR BEDROOM

The following three items, frequently found in the bedroom, can contribute to sleep, communication, and relationship problems.

Television

A TV set in the bedroom is a feng shui no-no! When it is positioned to be watched from the bed, the TV becomes a major focal point of the room, which means it will have a big effect on your relationship. If you absolutely must have a TV in the bedroom, hide it in an armoire or cover it with fabric at night, so you and your sweetie can focus on each other without commercial interruptions.

Your home office

When your home office is in the bedroom you may be tired and unfocused when you try to work, then unable to relax when it's time to sleep because work is so much on your mind. Sleep energy and work energy don't mix well. Ideally, your desk and your bed should each be in the command position; this is usually impossible to achieve when both are in the same room.

When relationships are a priority issue for you, it is even more important to find someplace else for your work area. If relocating your desk is impossible, find some way to disguise it at night, such as with a screen or an attractive piece of fabric.

Exercise equipment

Exercise equipment in the bedroom can turn your love life into a real workout. Don't even think about using the space underneath your bed for your workout gear; the exercise vibe will continue to disrupt your relationship and interfere with your ability to get a good night's sleep. Move your treadmill or free weights somewhere else; there are better ways to get a workout in the bedroom!

Remove Communication Blockers

One of the basic principles of feng shui is that little things can have a big effect on your life. Here are some seemingly minor household problems that could be affecting your ability to communicate openly and harmoniously with your partner.

FIGHTING DOORS

Doors that bump into each other when opened are called "fighting" doors in feng shui, and can lead to arguments. Often, the *gua* involved is reflected in the type of conflict you experience. Fighting doors in *kun gua*, for example, may lead to bickering about relationship issues. If closet doors "fight," conflicts may be hidden.

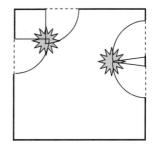

Cure fighting doors with red string or tassels. If you choose tassels, hang one from each doorknob. If using string, cut a piece long enough (in multiples of nine inches) to tie around both doorknobs when the doors are closed. Tie one end of the string to each doorknob, cut it in the middle, and wrap each loose end around the knob it hangs from. Be sure to use the body-speech-mind empowerment method as well.

FIRE-WATER CLASHES

FIRE and WATER fight each other: WATER puts out FIRE, but FIRE can also turn WATER to steam. A stove and sink directly opposite each other can lead to conflicts and arguments everywhere in the home, and especially in the kitchen. You can cure this situation by adding WOOD energy between the sink and the stove.

If you have a table or countertop between the sink and the stove, place a potted plant on it. If the space between sink and stove is open, place a green rug on the floor. If neither of these is possible, hang a faceted crystal ball halfway between the two and empower it to disrupt the conflicting _chi_—use red string cut to a multiple of nine inches to hang the crystal.

LOOSE OR TIGHT DOORKNOBS

If any of the doors (closet doors, too) in your relationship power spots have knobs that don't turn easily, it could be affecting your love life. Loose doorknobs can make it difficult to "get a grip" on a situation, and a doorknob that is too stiff can indicate difficulty making progress in whatever aspect of your life is indicated by the _gua_ in which that door is located. A stiff doorknob in a key area could also indicate you are feeling "uptight" about something there.

Take a few minutes to walk through your house, and check for loose or stiff doorknobs in key areas. Often all you need do is tighten a screw or two, or spritz a little WD-40® on it.

DIRTY WINDOWS

In feng shui, windows represent our ability to see things clearly. When your windows are dirty, your perception may be cloudy as well. When you don't see a situation clearly, you may become overly critical of your partner, or develop a tendency to jump to unwarranted conclusions. Or, perhaps your inability to see clearly has led you to fall in love with a person who isn't as wonderful as you think.

So, when was the last time you washed your windows—inside and out? As always, pay special attention to the windows in your romance power spots. Make sure that they are spotlessly clean so you can enjoy a clear perspective on your relationship.

Moving on...

Whether and when you move on to the next and final phase of the Relationship Cycle is very much up to you. For some people, no relationship will be a complete success without an exchange of vows and rings in a formal marriage ceremony. Other couples may be quite content maintaining separate homes and independent lives year after year, while regularly enjoying the companionship and romance of each other's company.

When the time is right, your decision to marry or share a home together moves you into the Uniting phase of the Relationship Cycle.

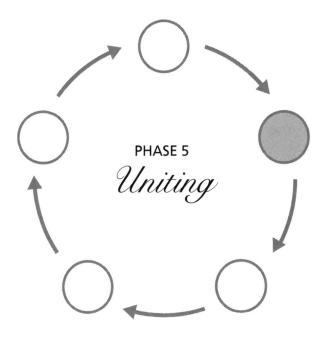

PHASE 5

Uniting

The final stage in your journey through the Relationship Cycle is Uniting. This is the stage of creating a shared home, as you and your partner decide to marry or move in together.

The focus of the Uniting stage is on forming a true partnership of mind, body, and spirit—issues that are beyond the scope of a book aimed at helping single people find romance. Approach this chapter as a brief preview of some of the issues and opportunities that await you as a couple, as well as some suggestions for how feng shui can help you make a smooth transition to living together. As you move forward into your life together, you can use what you've learned about feng shui throughout this book to assist you in your shared journey.

Before we begin, let's take a closer look at the qualities and characteristics of this stage from the perspective of feng shui.

The Earth Element in Feng Shui

The Uniting phase of the Relationship Cycle is associated with the EARTH element in feng shui. What comes to mind when you think about earth?

Earth is our foundation, our universal mother, that sense of home that we carry in our heart regardless of our relationship to the place of our birth. In feng shui, the EARTH element is associated with the transitional periods between the seasons: Indian summer, early spring, the time between autumn leaf-fall and the first snow, a pause when nature catches her breath as one season ends but the next has not yet fully begun.

EARTH has a settling energy. It is firm without being unyielding, stable without becoming stagnant. The earth colors are all the different shades of yellow and brown, as well as muted and "muddy" shades of orange.

In Traditional Chinese Medicine, EARTH is associated with the stomach; its sound is "singing." When in balance, EARTH energy is harmonious and nurturing. Problems with EARTH energy can lead to unwarranted worry and anxiety.

The "virtues" of EARTH are fairness, trust, and consideration, key qualities for any successful long-term relationship. When EARTH energy is healthy, you are a considerate and thoughtful caretaker of yourself as well as others. You can set appropriate boundaries, say "no" when necessary, and be comfortable receiving as well as giving.

When EARTH is too strong, you may become carried away by your urge to nurture, sacrificing your own needs to take care of others. When EARTH *chi* is weak, you become overwhelmed with selfishness, wanting to be cared for without the responsibility of caring for others.

JOURNALING

Find some quiet time to reflect on your personal experience of the EARTH phase in past relationships, and to think about how you have reacted to the challenges and opportunities of Uniting as you moved into this phase in the past.

• How do you usually respond to this phase, both emotionally and physically?

• What aspects of creating a stable, committed relationship come naturally to you? Which are difficult?

• Has trust, fairness, or consideration been an issue in any of your past relationships? What has that taught you about your own needs and behaviors?

• Do you draw appropriate boundaries in your relationships with others? Are you able to give and receive in equal measure?

• What insight, if any, have you gained from exploring EARTH energy from a feng shui perspective?

Think about what personal challenges are likely to surface for you in this phase of the relationship cycle. This might include standing up for your own need to be nurtured, rather than always being the caregiver for others. Learning to trust again may be a challenge for you, or perhaps your biggest opportunity is to fully earn the trust of others.

Earth Energy and the Ba Gua

You already know that the EARTH element is associated with *kun gua* (relationships). If I still have to show you on a diagram where *kun gua* is located, you haven't been paying attention (but you can look it up on page 23). EARTH is also the element of *ken gua* (self-understanding) and of the center of the *ba gua*, the *tai chi*.

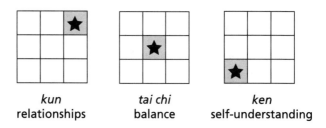

| *kun* | *tai chi* | *ken* |
| relationships | balance | self-understanding |

When you place the *ba gua* according to the compass directions, *kun gua* is in the southwest, and *ken gua* is in the northeast. The *tai chi* is always in the center.

From the perspective of the Uniting phase of the Relationship Cycle, *kun gua* has to do with discovering how to balance the nurturing and receptive qualities of a relationship. *Ken gua* has to do with maintaining a strong sense of self within the context of your relationship, and with the insight and perspective you gain from your spiritual practice.

EARTH is nourished by FIRE, so many of the changes you have made in the Loving phase will continue to support you now. Be aware that too much WOOD will disrupt EARTH, and METAL will deplete it, and make appropriate adjustments to your home.

Find Your "Uniting" Power Spots

Because we have arrived at the stage of marriage and commitment, your strongest Uniting power spots will be the *kun gua* power spots that you have been working with throughout this book. If your transition into the Uniting phase has involved moving into a new home or moving in with your partner, you will need to identify your *kun gua* power spots in your new home. (Turn back to pages 24-26 if you need to review the instructions on locating *kun gua* power spots in the home.)

The biggest shift in your situation now is that you are no longer using feng shui for yourself alone. You and/or your partner may have other issues that could appropriately be addressed now. You can use the *ba gua* grid as a template for reviewing life issues with your new partner:

how will we handle our money?	defining shared goals	wedding plans!
joining our two families	UNITING	visioning our future
private time/space; honoring boundaries	balancing our careers	community service

Feng Shui for the Uniting Phase

SYMBOLS OF FIDELITY

In traditional Chinese culture, a pair of cranes or mandarin ducks symbolize fidelity, honesty, and longevity. A pair of butterflies is another symbol of conjugal love. Any of these are an appropriate enhancements for your bedroom, front entry, or *kun gua* power spot.

GATHERING WEDDING CHI

Recently married couples are a wonderful source of auspicious wedding *chi*. You can acquire some of this good *chi* this way:

Gather nine small items that you either carry with you or use frequently, such as your house or car keys, a favorite pen, a ring, cufflinks, or other jewelry. These items should be personal, and permanent. For example, a lipstick would be a personal item for a lady, but because it eventually gets used up and discarded it is not appropriate for this cure. Small items with special meaning for you, such as a figurine, crystal, or amulet could also be used.

Wrap these nine items in a cloth, and ask the newlyweds to bless them, touching each of the objects, with the intention that you acquire some of their wedding *chi*. This should be done within 30 days of the wedding.

Gathering wedding *chi* in this way is a good way for couples to strengthen their relationship, and for singles to increase their luck in romance. If you and your partner are soon to be married, plan to share your wedding *chi* with your single friends.

THE IF-YOU'RE-DESPERATE CURE

If you are yearning for committment from someone who hasn't yet taken that important step, here's a feng shui ritual that may help.

You will need two photographs—one of you and one of your beloved—a brand new pen, and a very long piece of red string.

On the night of a full moon, sit in the moonlight (outdoors or where the moon shines in a window). Write your beloved's name on the back of your photo, and your name on the back of the other. Add the words:"happily married" to the back of each photo, and place the photos face to face.

Now, take your red string and wrap it around the photos 99 times while chanting *om mani padme hum* 99 times and focusing on your intention for commitment with this person.

Sleep with the photos under your pillow or between your box spring and mattress in the *kun gua* position (upper right corner at the pillow end of the bed) for nine nights. On the 10th day, take the string-wrapped packet and toss it into flowing water, such as a stream or river. Watch until it floats out of sight, visualizing the two of you going through life united together.

An important cautionary note: This ritual gets uncomfortably close to using feng shui for manipulative reasons, which is never a good idea. I strongly suggest, should you decide to use this cure, that you have a clear intention that the outcome be in the best possible interest of everyone involved. This means you must be willing to accept the *end* of this relationship if you are not truly meant to be together. Once you do this cure, muddling on as before is no longer an option.

Creating a Shared Home

SPACE CLEARING

The committment to sharing a home is a major turning point in your life. Whether you are moving into a new home together or one of you is moving in with the other, a space clearing ceremony (see pages 65-68) that you perform together is a wonderful way to energize your space and create a "clean slate" for your life together.

HOUSE BLESSING CEREMONY

A blessing ceremony for your shared home is a wonderful way to celebrate your commitment to creating a beautiful life together. The ceremony described here, called "Tracing the Nine Stars," balances and activates the *chi* of all nine *guas* and blesses the home with good luck. The new moon is an auspicious time to perform this ritual. If you can perform a space-clearing ceremony first, that's even better. This is a wonderful ceremony to do before you move your furniture and belongings into a new home.

Preparation

Be clear about your intention and reason(s) for doing the ceremony. Have nine red envelopes ready, and a small bowl of uncooked rice.

On nine small pieces of paper, write a wish or blessing for each of the eight outer *guas*, plus a special all-encompassing wish for the center of the home (the *tai chi*).

You and your partner may choose to write your wishes or blessings together, or you may each write a personal wish or blessing for each *gua* on a separate piece of paper. Either way, you will use nine red envelopes.

Blessing

Ring bells and light some incense to begin the ceremony. State your intentions aloud, along with an overall intention to bless the space.

Follow the nine-star path shown in the diagram below as you move through your space. In a multi-level home, try to include at least one area on each level in your path; for example, a bedroom on the second floor could be chosen for the *kun gua* blessing.

Beginning with *jen gua* (1), read the blessings or wishes you wrote down aloud, then put the paper(s) into a red envelope and add a few grains of the rice. Place the envelope somewhere in that area where it can remain in place for a while. Use the body-speech-mind empowerment method, visualizing your desired outcome.

hsun	li	kun
2	7	9
jen	**tai chi**	**dui**
1	3	5
ken	**kan**	**chien**
6	8	4

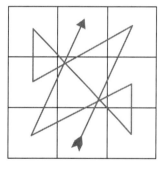

Move on to the next *gua*, read your wishes or blessings aloud, and do the red envelope thing. When all envelopes have been placed in the appropriate *gua*s, ring the bells again to close the ceremony.

Follow-Up

Leave the red envelopes in place for 27 days. On the 28th day (mark this date on a calendar, so you don't forget!), collect the envelopes and place them in a special place, such as a home altar, or burn them. If you burn the envelopes, use the body-speech-mind method to empower the smoke to carry your wishes and blessings to heaven.

Continuing the Journey

As you have now experienced firsthand, the Fast Feng Shui Relationship Cycle echoes the Creative cycle of the elements: METAL producing WATER, WATER nourishing WOOD, WOOD feeding FIRE, FIRE turning to EARTH, EARTH creating METAL, and then around again. As you and your partner build a life together, your understanding of these energies can go on inspiring and supporting you.

Now that you have united with your partner, your issues and concerns shift to the many other life aspirations addressed by feng shui: children and family, career and finances, self-knowledge, and that all-important—and often elusive—quality addressed in the *tai chi* at the center of your home: life balance.

I am delighted at your success in romance, and hope that in your journey beyond the scope of this book you will continue to make feng shui an integral part of your life. You can stay in touch and learn about forthcoming titles in the Fast Feng Shui Series at www.fastfengshui.com.

As always, I welcome your comments and feedback on this book; I would love to hear about your experiences and successes with using feng shui to enhance your love life and attract romance. You can write to me at stephanie@fastfengshui.com, or by mail at:

Lotus Pond Press
415 Dairy Road, Suite E-144
Kahului, Maui, HI 96732-2398

www.fastfengshui.com

Appendices

Appendix A.
Working with the Ba Gua

The *ba gua* (*ba*: eight; *gua*: area) is a map of the energetic world. It is traditionally shown as an octagon with eight sections surrounding a central area, the *tai chi*. For practical use, we extend the corners of the *ba gua* to form a square, then divide it into nine equal sections.

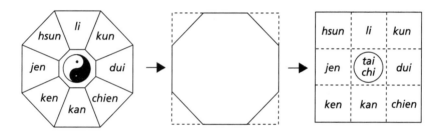

The *ba gua* divides any space into these nine areas. Each area corresponds to a different aspect of your life (see the diagram on the next page). Whatever is going on energetically—good or bad—in that part of your space will affect the related part of your life.

Every space has a *ba gua*. There is a *ba gua* for your plot of land, a *ba gua* for your house or apartment, and a *ba gua* for each room within your home. You can even apply the *ba gua* to your desk, bed, or stove.

Meanings of the Ba Gua

The *ba gua* is rich with meanings and associations. The primary meanings of the *guas* are shown in the chart on the next page. You do not need to learn the Chinese names, but they are a good reminder that each *gua* has many meanings.

For example, it's easy to think of *kan gua* as the "career" area, but it is also about making social connections—which means it becomes an important area for feng shui enhancements when you want to meet someone new.

When we use feng shui for romance, *kun gua* (relationships, and especially marriage) gets a lot of attention! However, all of the *guas* are important, and each one has its supporting role in helping you find lasting love and happiness.

WEALTH (hsun) Abundance Fortunate blessings Your ability to receive	FAME (li) Your reputation What you are famous (or infamous) for	RELATIONSHIPS (kun) Marriage Partnerships Everything feminine Your mother
FAMILY (jen) New beginnings Your ability to initiate Health Community	HEALTH (tai chi) Life balance (whatever happens here affects all guas)	CREATIVITY (dui) Your children Your ability to complete things
SELF-UNDERSTANDING (ken) Knowledge & learning Your spiritual life Self-awareness	CAREER (kan) Your life path Communication Social connections Wisdom	HELPFUL FRIENDS (chien) Benefactors/mentors Support systems Travel Your father

meanings of the *ba gua*

Placement of the Ba Gua

To place the *ba gua* energy map on your property, place the bottom edge on the side of your plot where the driveway meets the street. The street end of your driveway will be in self-understanding (*ken*), career (*kan*), or helpful friends (*chien*). Stretch the *ba gua* sideways and lengthwise to cover the entire property. It will probably end up as a rectangle rather than a square. That's okay.

What *gua* is your house in? Where is *kun gua* (relationships) on your property?

To apply the *ba gua* to your home, align the bottom edge with the wall your front door is in. Even if you usually enter your home through the garage or a back or side door, always align the *ba gua* to the front door. Now, stretch (or shrink) the *ba gua* to cover your entire space.

To apply the *ba gua* to an individual room, do the same thing: align the *ba gua* with the doorway wall, and adjust the size to fit the space. As you stand in the doorway facing into the space, *kun gua* (relationships) is always to the far right.

If there is more than one way to enter a space, orient the *ba gua* to the most prominent entryway. If the entries are equal, choose the one that is more frequently used.

The *ba gua* for each floor above or below the main floor is aligned to where you enter that level from the top (for higher floors) or bottom (for lower floors) of the stairs. Sometimes there will be a wall directly in front of you at the top or bottom of the stairs, and you will need to turn to the right or left before you are facing into the space.

With a recessed entry, parts of the room or building will be behind you as you face into the space from the doorway. These areas are extensions of *ken* (self understanding), *kan* (career), and/or *chien* (helpful friends) *guas*.

Extensions and Missing Areas in Kun Gua

EXTENSIONS

An extension is a part of the home that sticks out from the rest of the structure. The part that sticks out must be less than one-half the total length or width of that side of the house or room to be considered an extension.

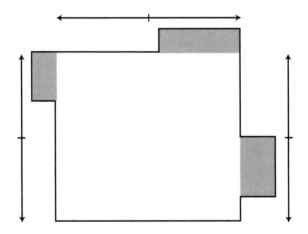

An extension means that the energy of that *gua* is very strong. Take a look at the areas you circled on your floor plans—any extentions in a power spot mean that the feng shui enhancements you place there will be very powerful.

MISSING AREAS

A missing area is a place where there is a "bite" out of the floor plan of your home. This gap must be less than one-half the total length or width of that side of the house or room to be considered missing.

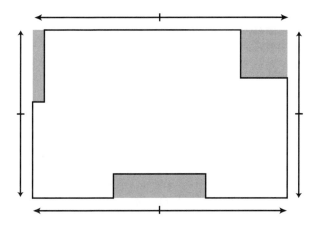

A missing area in a *gua* means that the energy of that *gua* is weak. If there is a missing area in any of your power spots, you will want to use feng shui to correct it.

Details on how to correct a missing *kun gua* can be found in the chapter about Phase 3 of the Relationship Cycle. You can use these same methods to correct a missing area in any of the *guas*.

The Ba Gua and Compass Directions

Sometimes you will see the *ba gua* labeled with compass directions, with north at *kan* (career), and south at *li* (fame). In the Chinese system north is at the bottom, and south is at the top, which is the opposite of how most of us are accustomed to seeing maps.

This makes sense when you understand that north is associated with winter, darkness, stillness, cold, and midnight, and that south is associated with summer, brightness, movement, heat, and midday. When energy is cold and still, it settles; warm, active energy rises.

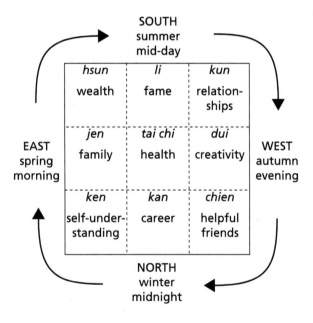

East is at the left side of the *ba gua*, associated with springtime, increasing light, warmth, growth, and morning. West, on the right, is associated with autumn, lessening light, cooling, decay, and twilight. Thus the *ba gua* describes the ever-changing, never-ending cycle of birth, growth, decay, death, and rebirth.

In traditional Chinese feng shui, the *ba gua* is aligned according to the compass directions, and you may see it used that way in some books and magazines. This can be confusing, because in Western feng shui the *ba gua* is always aligned with the entry, so *kun gua* (relationships) is always the far right corner when you stand in the doorway facing into the space.

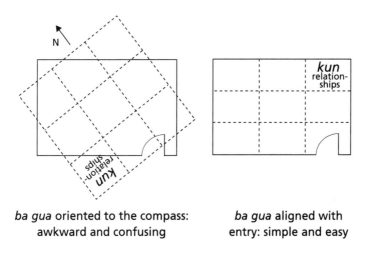

<table>
<tr><td>

ba gua oriented to the compass:
awkward and confusing

</td><td>

ba gua aligned with
entry: simple and easy

</td></tr>
</table>

Fast Feng Shui places the *ba gua* according to the entry. In my years of practice—both with clients and in my own life—I have found this approach to be admirably simple and effective.

If you are concerned that by ignoring the compass directions you may be leaving something out, here's what you can do. First, apply the *ba gua* to your home by aligning it with your front door. Then, look at the compass directions. If there is close alignment of the two *ba guas*, you will know that any changes you make in each *gua* will be even more effective. If the two *ba guas* are very misaligned, keep in mind that your "cures" may need to work a little harder.

You can also look at how the two sets of *guas* overlap when you place the *ba gua* different ways. For example, place the *ba gua* on your floor plan according to your front door, then look for *kun gua*, the area associated with marriage and relationships. Now, look at the compass direction of that corner of the home, and look up the *gua* associated with that direction in the chart on the next page.

COMPASS	GUA	MEANING
North	*kan*	career, social connections
Northeast	*ken*	self-understanding, spirituality
East	*jen*	family, community, health
Southeast	*hsun*	wealth, fortunate blessings
South	*li*	fame, reputation
Southwest	*kun*	relationships, romance
West	*dui*	creativity, children
Northwest	*chien*	helpful friends, travel

Now, find the southwest area, which is associated with *kun gua* (relationships) on the compass. What other *gua* does it overlap with when you use the doorway orientation?

Think of the compass direction as adding a second layer of understanding to your *ba gua*. For example, if your *kun gua* is in the eastern corner of your home (associated with family), that's a great place for feng shui remedies to ease family tensions that may be related to your love life.

Remember, if you find the compass directions confusing, or don't want to deal with another layer of detail, it's perfectly okay to leave them out. None of the cures and strategies in this book rely on the compass, although suggestions for incorporating the compass directions are included throughout as an optional aspect of your feng shui work.

In Fast Feng Shui, our primary focus is on creating a harmonious flow of *chi* through your space, creating an environment that welcomes and supports romance, and with using the symbolic power of your imagery to support and enhance your progress.

Appendix B.
The Cycles of the Elements

The five elements describe five essential qualities of *chi*, which you can use to enhance, control, or balance a space, depending on your needs:

- METAL—the quality of contraction, sharpness, focus; when too strong, can make you sharp-tongued and critical

- WATER—the quality of flowing, making connections; too much can make you "wishy-washy" and indecisive

- WOOD—the quality of upward growth, easy progress; too much can make you aggressive or impatient, lacking in compassion

- FIRE—the quality of excitement, expansion, quickness; too much can leave you stressed out and anxious

- EARTH—the quality of settling down, being receptive; too much leads to depression, sluggishness, feeling stuck or weighed down

Each element can help shift your energy and/or the energy of your space, and you can use this when you address relationship issues. METAL helps you concentrate and get things done; its inward focus helps you reassess a situation when you need to let go of a relationship that has ended. WATER is helpful when things have been stuck for a while (think of ice melting), and for improving communication, so it's helpful when you decide to start dating again. WOOD energy is associated with new beginnings, and it can help you make smooth progress in a new relationship. FIRE creates heat and action, and is the energy to use when you want to increase passion and intensity. EARTH energy is good when you need more stability in a relationship, or are dealing with issues of commitment.

The Fast Feng Shui Relationship Cycle uses these qualities of chi to coordinate feng shui advice and tactics to the specific needs of each stage of the cycle.

Element Shapes and Colors

Each element is associated with specific shapes and colors:

- METAL—white, gold, silver, grey; round and oval shapes, arches
- WATER—black and dark blues; sinuous, curvy, irregular, and wave-like shapes
- WOOD—greens and light blues; tall narrow shapes
- FIRE—reds, purples, bright oranges; triangles, flame shapes and other pointed or angular shapes
- EARTH—browns, yellows, cool or muted oranges; low, flat, square shapes

This is the basic information that you can use to adjust the energy of specific rooms and areas of your home. For example, to spice up your relationship areas, add more FIRE energy: things that are red, pink, and/or triangular in shape.

The material that something is made of is important, too. Some obvious examples are:

- Brass clock—METAL
- Fish tank—WATER
- Houseplants and flowers—WOOD
- Electric lights—FIRE
- Pottery bowl—EARTH

Others are not so obvious. A mahogany dining table, for example, is made out of wood, but it is square, flat, and (unless it's been painted) brown in color. In energetic terms, then, it has more EARTH energy than WOOD energy, because the wood is no longer vital and growing, and the shape and color of the table are associated with EARTH. A candle is a good example of the FIRE element, but if it is a tall green candle it also has WOOD energy because of its shape and color.

Many items have a combination of qualities, so you will need to use your best judgment about how much of what kind of influence it will have on your space. Try not to go nuts puzzling over what element something represents. If it's not clear right away, then chances are good it combines several different qualities and will not have as strong an impact on your space.

Keep in mind that function, placement, and your own intention are important, too. If you worry so much about choosing the right elements that you no longer enjoy your possessions, you're trying too hard! Feng shui should be easy, graceful, and fun. If you love something, it has good *chi* for you. And as you progress through this book you'll learn where to put it.

Element Cycles: How the Energies Interact

The five elements interact with each other in very specific ways. This enables you to be more sophisticated and flexible in your use of the elements as you feng shui your home and your love life. For example, to increase the FIRE energy in a space, you can feed it by adding WOOD. Too much FIRE going on? Add WATER to cool it down. Once you understand these different interactions, you'll always know what element to use where and why—so read on!

THE CREATIVE CYCLE

Each of the five elements is nourished, supported, or "fed" by one of the other elements. This forms a sequence called the Creative cycle (also called the Productive cycle), as shown in the diagram below.

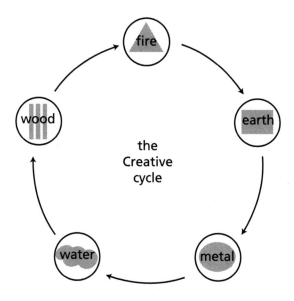

Here's how it works:

- METAL produces WATER (think of moisture condensing on a cold can of soda on a hot day)

- WATER nourishes WOOD (without water, wood will die)

- WOOD feeds FIRE (without fuel, fire cannot burn)

- FIRE creates EARTH (as the fire burns, it produces a pile of ashes; think of a volcano becoming a mountain)

- EARTH produces METAL (metal is extracted from the earth)

Use the Creative cycle when you want to increase the effect of an element in a particular space.

THE REDUCING CYCLE

As each element feeds or nourishes the next in the Creative cycle, its own energy is reduced by the effort. For example, you can counteract the strong WATER energy in a bathroom by adding WOOD energy to the space (green towels, for example). This gives the WATER something to do (feeding WOOD), reduces its strength, and helps bring things back into balance. Here's how the Reducing cycle works:

* METAL reduces EARTH

* EARTH reduces FIRE

* FIRE reduces WOOD

* WOOD reduces WATER

* WATER reduces METAL

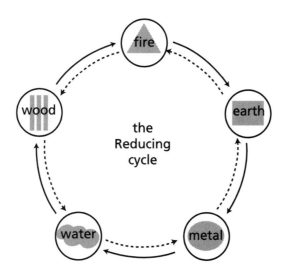

Use the Reducing cycle when you want a gentle way to bring a situation into better balance. It's easy to remember the Reducing cycle if you know the Creative cycle; just keep in mind that when one element nourishes another one, its own energy is reduced by the effort.

THE CONTROLLING CYCLE

When one element is very strong, you may need something stronger than the reducing effect to bring it back into balance. This is where the Controlling cycle comes in handy. The Controlling cycle works like this:

- METAL chops WOOD

- WOOD breaks up EARTH (think of a new crop pushing up through the soil, or of tree roots pushing down into the earth)

- EARTH dams or muddies WATER

- WATER puts out FIRE

- FIRE melts METAL

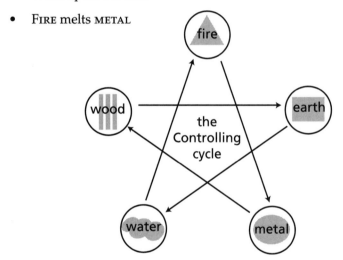

Make sure the controlling element is strong and supported. If you try to put out a bonfire with a tea-cup full of water, the water will evaporate without having much effect. Keep in mind that:

- Too much METAL can overwhelm FIRE

- Too much FIRE evaporates WATER

- Too much WATER can wash EARTH away

- Too much EARTH can smother WOOD

- Too much WOOD can take the edge off METAL

Putting it all Together

The key to working with the elements is to focus on which effect you want to have in a specific space or situation:

- If you want to increase the strength of an element, add the two elements that come before it in the Creative cycle. For example, if you want to increase FIRE energy, add WATER and WOOD to the space. The WATER will feed the WOOD, which will enhance FIRE. You don't have to worry about the WATER reducing FIRE, because its energy is being diverted to create WOOD:

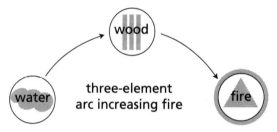

- If you want to decrease the strength of an element, use the Controlling cycle *or* the two elements that follow it in the Creative cycle:

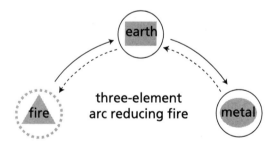

If FIRE energy is too strong, adding EARTH and METAL energy will reduce the energy of FIRE.

Using three elements in this way is more powerful than just using one or two. Get in the habit of thinking in threes when you work with the elements, and your feng shui cures will be much more effective.

The Elements and the Ba Gua

Each *gua* is associated with one of the elements, as shown below. There are three EARTH *guas* (including the *tai chi*), two WOOD and METAL *guas*, and one *gua* each for WATER and FIRE. The element of each *gua* determines the color associated with it.

Jen gua (family) is pale green; darker greens are associated with *hsun gua* (wealth). *Hsun gua* is also associated with the color purple, because that color is symbolic of wealth.

Kun gua, the relationship area, is red, pink, and white, because it is located between *li gua* (fame; red) and *dui gua* (creativity; white), and because pink is the color of romance.

The color of *chien gua*, (helpful friends; METAL) is grey, because it is located between the pure white *dui gua* and the black of *kan gua* (career; WATER).

hsun	*li*	*kun*
wealth	fame	relationships
WOOD green & purple	FIRE red	EARTH pink
jen	*tai chi*	*dui*
family	health	creativity
WOOD green	EARTH yellow	METAL white
ken	*kan*	*chien*
self-understanding	career	helpful friends
EARTH brown	WATER black	METAL white & grey

Each element is naturally strong in some *guas* and weak in others, information that you can use to fine-tune your feng shui adjustments. See the Five Elements Reference Chart on the next page for details.

FIVE ELEMENT REFERENCE CHART

Element	Qualities	Colors	Shapes	Strong in	Weak in	Creates	Reduces	Controls	Controlled by
WOOD	uplifting growing initiating	greens light blues	tall narrow upright	jen hsun kan	dui chien li	fire	water	earth	metal
FIRE	active radiating empowering	reds purples hot orange	triangles pointed sharp	li jen hsun	kan ken kun	earth	wood	metal	water
EARTH	settling grounding stabilizing	browns yellows beiges	square rectangles flat hollow	ken kun tai chi li	jen hsun dui chien	metal	fire	water	wood
METAL	focused internalizing analyzing	white gold & silver metallics	round oval curved arcs	dui chien ken kun	li kan	water	earth	wood	fire
WATER	flowing connecting communicating	black dark blue	wavy irregular sinuous	kan dui chien	ken kun jen hsun	wood	metal	fire	earth

My Personal Ba Gua for Phase: ___

Photocopy this page for the activities in
Phases 1-5 of the Relationship Cycle.

Wealth (*hsun*)	Fame (*li*)	Relationships (*kun*)
Family (*jen*)	Health (*tai chi*)	Creativity (*dui*)
Self-Understanding (*ken*)	Career (*kan*)	Helpful Friends (*chien*)

My priority *guas* for this phase are:

1. _____

2. _____

3. _____

Appendix C.
Feng Shui Objects & How to Use Them

FENG SHUI CRYSTALS

Faceted crystal balls are a very popular feng shui cure. In addition to energizing a space, their ability to refract a beam of light (and *chi*) and send it radiating in all directions makes it an ideal protection against *sha* (negative) *chi*.

These crystal balls can also be used to empower and activate a space. They radiate blessings wherever they are placed, and are powerful magnifiers of your intention.

Faceted crystal balls can be used anywhere you want to enhance *chi*. Good places to hang crystal balls include:

- In the center of a long, narrow hallway

- In front of a window through which too much *chi* is escaping

- Anywhere you'd like to activate *chi*

Crystals are most often hung from the ceiling, a doorway, or in windows. For added impact, hang your crystal ball from a red string or ribbon cut to a multiple of nine inches (9", 18", 27"). The ball can hang any distance from the ceiling; it's the cut length of the string that is important. Tie any extra string into a nice bow or decorative knot. If you buy crystal balls from a feng shui supplier, they may come with red cord already attached.

You can also place a faceted crystal ball on a desk, table, or home altar. Wear a little one on a red ribbon around your neck to activate your personal *chi*, or hang one from the rear-view mirror of your car to enhance, bless, and protect you while you drive.

WIND CHIMES

The sound waves created by a wind chime will slow down and help disperse *chi* that is moving too quickly. If the path from the street to your front door is long and straight, hang a wind chime by the door or porch steps to slow the *chi* down so it enters your home gently.

Wind chimes are also good for lifting the energy of a space. If one corner of your yard is lower than the others, *chi* may settle there. Hanging a wind chime from a tree in that corner can stir the *chi* up and keep it moving.

Wind chimes come in many sizes, from tinkly little tiny ones to great big resonant ones. Match the size of the wind chime to the size of your space. A large brass wind chime might be overwhelming indoors, while a very small chime may not be strong enough to have much effect. Choose metal chimes, as they have the most penetrating tone. The most important consideration for a wind chime is that the sound be pleasing to you, so pick the one whose tones you like the best.

WATER FOUNTAINS

In feng shui terms, moving water brings prosperity and good luck to the home. The sound and motion of gurgling water activates *chi* and adds humidity to a dry room, helping to balance *chi*. Moving water gets things going when the *chi* has been stagnant for a while (think of ice melting in the spring). Use moving water cures anywhere you want to enhance WATER or WOOD energy.

Water fountains come in many shapes and sizes; pick one that:

- Suits the style of your décor

- Is an appropriate size for the place you intend to use it

- Incorporates the materials, shapes, and/or colors of the element energies you want to add to that space

You can usually adjust the sound of a water fountain by changing the water level. Some fountains also come with an adjustable pump, so you can vary the speed with which the water flows. Experiment until you find a tone and volume that sounds right.

Be sure to add more water to your fountain as it evaporates, to avoid possible damage to the pump if the water level gets too low. Depending on your climate and the size of the fountain, this could be once a week or every day. If you will be away from home for several days, unplug the fountain while you are gone.

If you place an outdoor fountain by your front door to activate *kan gua* (career), make sure the water flows toward your door, not away from it. You want all that good *chi* to come into your life, not flow out of it! Indoors, place the fountain so the water flow is directed toward the interior of the home, rather than toward the front door.

Some people find the sound of a water fountain distracting, and a fountain is generally not recommended for the bedroom, unless you turn it off while you are sleeping. Be guided by your personal response, and choose another cure if a fountain isn't right for you.

AQUARIUMS

An aquarium can be extremely effective at increasing wealth and luck. Both the water pump and the fish swimming around in it keep the water moving and the *chi* going strong.

The best places for an aquarium are in *kan* (career) and *hsun* (wealth) *guas*, or near the front door. Combine eight orange fish and one black one, or eight black fish and one gold one. If you are using an aquarium to increase wealth, add nine coins to the tank.

Be sure to keep your fish tank immaculately clean. Less-than-fresh water and algae-clogged filters won't do your fish any good, and will send yucky-water *chi* out into the room. If any of your fish die, replace them immediately with bigger, more expensive ones.

MIRRORS

Mirrors have been called "the aspirin of feng shui" because they solve so many feng shui probems. By creating the visual experience of a larger, deeper, or wider space, mirrors energetically enhance and expand a room or *gua*. For this reason, they are the best way to correct a missing gua from inside the space (see pages 141-144 for details of this use).

Mirrors can also be placed to correct a narrow or blocked entryway (see pages 116-117), and to help brighten up any space that is too dark. Mirrors are especially useful for providing you with a view of the doorway to a room, when it is impossible to place a key piece of furniture—such as your bed, desk, or stove—in the command position (see pages 83-84). You can also use a mirror to reflect something with good *chi* (such as a beautiful pond or a lush green tree outside a window) into an indoor area, to enhance that space.

If there is a bathroom in one of your power spots, hang a full-length mirror on the outside of the door and empower it to prevent *chi* from entering the bathroom, where it may be depleted by the draining effect of all that plumbing.

If you can hang a mirror on the wall above your stove so that it reflects the burners, this is thought to symbolically double your income and prosperity.

When you choose to hang a mirror in your home, always check to see what's reflected in it, to make sure it is doubling something with positive energy. Avoid hanging a mirror so that the top of your head is cut off in the reflection; this can cause self-image problems, and may give you a headache.

Small round mirrors (1"-6" in diameter") are also useful in feng shui. Place one under a personal power object to enhance its energy. You can also write a wish on a slip of paper, place it between two mirrors (reflective sides together), and empower the mirrors to multiply the power of your wish and help it to come true. I am so fond of this particular cure that I have designed a unique new product, called feng Wish Books specifically for this purpose. These hand-crafted "books" have small mirrors inset into the inside covers to enhance a written wish placed between them. They are available at www.fastfengshui.com.

LIGHT

Poorly lit rooms have dull, depressing *chi*. If your power spots are dim and dark, your feng shui cures will have to work harder to achieve the desired effect. If you want to enhance your love life, make sure the lighting in your bedroom is romantic. Activate a power spot within that room with a pink lightbulb. Here are some other ways to use lights:

- Put a bright light anywhere you want to lift or activate *chi*

- Drape a string of little lights over a large houseplant

- Use a bright light anywhere you want to strengthen the FIRE or EARTH elements, or to control METAL

- Place a bright light in a *li gua* (fame; illumination) power spot if one of your goals is to understand a situation better

- Use a spotlight to emphasize the significant imagery you have chosen for a key position in a power spot

- Use an uplight on the floor in a power spot with a slanted ceiling, or under an overhead beam

- Use a timer to activate a light cure each night between 11 PM and 1 AM—so long as it will not disturb you or your neighbors

CHI-ACTIVATORS

Colorful flags fluttering in the breeze are a great way to stir up *chi*. If you have an exterior power spot, consider activating it with a flag, banner or whirly-gig. Flag poles, tree branches, eaves, and porch columns can all carry a flag or windsock. Choose shapes and colors based on the appropriate elements for added impact.

Mobiles and whirly-gigs can be used to enhance *chi* inside your home. Look for a mobile with imagery that supports your intentions; angels or stars are always good for blessing a space, for example. Check home and toy stores as well as feng shui suppliers for wind-powered *chi*-activators that appeal to you. If you use this type of cure in a place where there is not much air current, set it in motion manually from time to time as you walk by.

PLANTS AND FLOWERS

You can enhance the *chi* of your garden by planting flowers that correspond to the different *guas*. For example, any flower with white, pink, or red blossoms will enhance *kun gua* (relationships) in your garden or on your property. If you decide to use feng shui in your garden, be sure you select plants that are appropriate to your climate and landscape.

Garden feng shui is a complete topic of study all on its own. In addition to plant selection and garden layout, it includes:

- Creating a harmonious balance of sunshine and shadow

- Shape and placement of paths, trees, and flower beds

- Appropriate paving and ground-cover materials

- Selection and placement of water features such as streams, ponds, waterfalls or water fountains

- Selection and placement of garden accessories, such as bird baths, benches, trellises, and the like

Indoors, plants and flowers are among the most powerful of feng shui cures, because their living _chi_ brings natural vitality into your home. Of course, they only bring good _chi_ so long as the plants and flowers are healthy. Be sure to get rid of any failing plants or wilting flowers before they have an adverse effect on your space!

Choose flowers with blossoms that match the element associated with the _gua_ you are enhancing. Use flowers with pink blossoms for the bedroom or _kun gua_ (relationships), red or purple for _hsun_ (wealth) and _li_ (fame) _guas_, white for _dui_ (creativity) or _chien_ (helpful friends) _guas_, dark blue blossoms for _kan_ (career), and yellow or orange flowers for _ken_ (self-understanding).

As you plan where to use plants and flowers in your home, look for ways to use them in multiples of three and nine (feng shui power numbers). Some ways you can do this include:

- Place three or nine small plants or vases together in one spot

- Put three or nine blossoms in a vase

- Use three of the same kind of plant, and place one in each of three power spots

Remember that you can use artificial plants in any spot where there is insufficient light for a living plant. Avoid dried flowers, which no longer have any living energy.

STONES AND STATUES

Stones, boulders, and statues are all good for stabilizing fast-moving *chi* with their weight. Place a large boulder in your front yard if your house is very close to a busy street, to keep all that rushing *chi* from draining the vitality from your property. Indoors, a heavy statue or object placed near a window can serve the same function.

MUSIC

Music can lift your spirits, put you in a good (or bad!) mood, get you going at the start of the day, and help you relax at the end of it—all by shifting the *chi* of your space. If you want to bring more harmony to a relationship, you can enhance your other feng shui cures by playing more harmonious, romantic music—especially in the bedroom.

BELLS

Bells are most often used in feng shui where there is a need for some kind of warning or protection. If you are unable to put your bed in the command position (pages 83-84), for example, you can hang a bell on your bedroom door to alert you when someone enters. You can also hang a bell wherever you would like to energize or enhance the space.

Bells are rung to signal the beginning and end of ceremonies and meditation practices. The sound of the bell penetrates the space, and signals a shift in the energy. Bells are also a powerful tool used in space clearing rituals (see pages 65-68). Sometimes a combination of metals is used to create a more powerful energetic effect. Tibetan prayer bells are forged from seven metals, and are often decorated with important symbols to enhance their energy.

Bells come in all kinds of shapes and sizes, with or without handles and clappers. The type of bell you choose will depend on how and where you plan to use it. Again, be sure that the tone of the bell is pleasing to you—the quality of the sound is more important than the design. If you are hanging a bell on a string, use a red cord, string, or ribbon cut to a multiple of nine inches.

POWER OBJECTS

Firecrackers, fu dogs, talismans, and images of saints or deities are just a few examples of power objects that can protect you from negative energy. (See pages 85-86 for ideas of how to use power objects.)

In addition to the traditional feng shui power objects, any item or image that has strong protective energy for you can be used as a feng shui cure in your home. Be sure to use the body-speech-mind empowerment method (pages 10-12) with power object cures.

Creating A Personal Ritual or Ceremony

Bring a sense of the sacred to your feng shui practice with a ritual or ceremony to accompany the activation of your power spots. You can place your feng shui cures as part of a ceremony, or perform a ritual after the cures are in place. Perform your ritual for 3, 9, or 27 days for best effect. If your initial ceremony is an elaborate one, you may want to simplify your follow-up rituals by just repeating a few key actions on the subsequent days.

INGREDIENTS FOR A FENG SHUI CEREMONY

Here are some things you can include in your ceremony or ritual. You can embellish a home altar with some of the following items and leave them in place for 3, 9, or 27 days—or permanently.

- A piece of gorgeous brocade, silk, satin, or velvet cloth
- Votive candles, saints candles
- Incense
- Bells
- Fresh flowers (remove as soon as they start to wilt)
- Coins or paper currency (roll paper money into a cylinder and tie with a red ribbon; coins should be in multiples of 3 or 9)
- Religious symbols, images, or statues
- Photographs of people significant to you
- Small red envelopes (to hold written wishes or blessings)
- Water, wine, or spirits
- Music
- Uncooked rice (a few grains or a small bowlful)
- Natural crystals
- Other objects from nature (feathers, rocks, shells, etc.)
- Personal power objects or mementos

BASIC PROCEDURE

Ring a bell to begin and end your ceremony. Build the core of your ritual around the three steps of the empowerment process:

1. Use the power of **body**—Perform a physical action such as lighting a candle, placing a flower in a vase, writing a wish on a slip of paper and putting it into a red envelope, or holding a specific *mudra* (hand gesture) for a few moments.

2. Use the power of **speech**—Say a prayer, sing a hymn, chant a *mantra* (such as *om mani padme hum*), or state your wishes aloud.

3. Use the power of **mind**—Focus on a specific intention or desire, or imagine your home (or a specific *gua*) filled with golden light and infinite blessings; feel as though all your desires have been fulfilled, so that your heart is full and joyful.

SUCCESS TIPS

- Make sure you have all of the items you need at hand.

- Choose a quiet time when you are not likely to be distracted or interrupted, and when you won't feel rushed.

- Invite other family members to perform the ceremony with you, if appropriate.

- Go with the flow: if you feel moved to add something new in the middle of the ceremony (or to skip something you had planned to do), honor that feeling; allow yourself to be spontaneous.

- Take your ritual or ceremony seriously, without becoming rigid or uptight about it; you are blessing and celebrating your home, so be expansive in spirit! Dancing, singing, and joyful laughter are just as appropriate as quiet contemplation, so do whatever feels right for you.

Appendix D.
Feng Shui Resources

In addition to the information provided here,
you will find many other resources through the links page at
www.fastfengshui.com

Books & Videos

This is a personal list, based on my own reading and practice. It is
by nature incomplete and is sure to omit many deserving titles.

TRADITIONAL CHINESE FENG SHUI

Lillian Too, *Feng Shui Fundamentals: Love,* Element Books, 1997;
The Illustrated Encyclopedia of Feng Shui, Element Books, 2000

Eva Wong, *Feng Shui: The Ancient Wisdom of Harmonious Living
for Modern Times,* Shambala, 1996; *A Master Course in Feng
Shui,* Shambala, 2001

CONTEMPORARY WESTERN FENG SHUI
The first book in the Fast Feng Shui series provides a quick and
easy introduction to the basic principles of western feng shui:

Stephanie Roberts, *Fast Feng Shui: 9 Simple Principles for
Transforming Your Life by Energizing Your Home,* Lotus Pond
Press, 2001

The following titles are among my favorites for beginners:

Terah Kathryn Collins, *The Western Guide to Feng Shui: Creating
Balance, Harmony and Prosperity in Your Environment,* Hay
House, 1996

Jami Lin, *Feng Shui Today, Earth Design the Added Dimension,* Earth
Design, 1995; *Personalized Consultation* workbook series

Denise Linn, *Feng Shui for the Soul,* Hay House, 2000

William Spear, *Feng Shui Made Easy: Designing Your Life with the
Ancient Art of Placement,* HarperSanFrancisco, 1995

Angel Thompson, *Feng Shui: how to Achieve the Most Harmonious Arrangement of Your Home and Office*, St. Martin's Griffin, 1996

Nancilee Wydra, *Designing Your Happiness: A Contemporary Look at Feng Shui*, Heian, 1995

I like these for their case-study approach and exquisite photographs:

R.D. Chin, *Feng Shui Revealed*, Clarkson N. Potter, 1998

Gina Lazenby, *The Feng Shui House Book*, Watson Guptill, 1998

For an in-depth look at the use of color in feng shui:

Sarah Rossbach, *Living Color: Master Lin Yun's Guide to Feng Shui and the Art of Color*, Kodasha, 1994

For a holistic approach to home design:

Robin Lennon, *Home Design from the Inside Out: Feng Shui, Color Therapy, and Self-Awareness*, Penguin USA, 1997

JOURNALING

Sheila Bender, *A Year in the Life: Journaling for Self-Discovery*, Writers Digest Books, 2000

Eldonna Bouton, *Journaling from the Heart*, Whole Heart Productions, 2000

Joyce Chapman, *Journaling for Joy*, Newcastle, 1991

CLUTTER CLEARING

Karen Kingston, *Clear Your Clutter with Feng Shui*, Broadway, 1999

Michelle Passoff, *Lighten Up! Free Yourself from Clutter*, Harper Collins, 1998

VISUALIZATION

Sonia Choquette, *Your Heart's Desire*, Three Rivers Press, 1997

Shakti Gawain, *Creative Visualization*, New World Library, 1995

Lynn Grabhorn, *Excuse Me, Your Life is Waiting*, Hampton Roads, 2000

LOVE & RELATIONSHIPS

John Amadeo, *The Authentic Heart: An Eightfold Path to Midlife Love*, John Wiley & Sons, 2001

Arthur Clark and Cassandra Skouras, *Finding Your Perfect Love,* Rosebud Press, 1998

Eve Hogan, *Virtual Foreplay: A Guide to Meeting and Dating Online*, Hunter House, 2001

Patricia Joudry, *Twin Souls: Finding Your True Spiritual Partner,* Hazelden Information Education, 2000

Don Miguel Ruiz, *The Mastery of Love: A Practical Guide to the Art of Relationship*, Amber Allen, 1999

SPACE CLEARING & SACRED SPACES

Karen Kingston, *Creating Sacred Space with Feng Shui*, Broadway, 1997

Denise Linn, *Space Clearing: How to Purify and Create Harmony in Your Home*, Contemporary Books, 2000; *Sacred Space: Clearing and Enhancing the Energy in Your Home*, Ballantine, 1996

Peg Streep, *Altars Made Easy: A Complete Guide to Creating Your Own Sacred Space*, HarperSanFrancisco, 1997

GARDEN FENG SHUI

Gill Hale, *The Complete Guide to the Feng Shui Garden*, Storey Books, 1998

Nancilee Wydra, *Feng Shui in the Garden*, NTC Contemporary, 1998

TRADITIONAL CHINESE MEDICINE & QIGONG

Harriet Beinfield & Efrem Korngold, *Between Heaven and Earth: A Guide to Chinese Medicine*, Ballantine, 1992

Roger Jahnke, *The Healer Within*, HarperSanFrancisco, 1999

Ted J. Kaputchuk, *The Web That Has No Weaver, Understanding Chinese Medicine*, Contemporary Books, 2000

MEDITATION, SPIRITUALITY, CONSCIOUS LIVING...

Martha Nibley Beck, *Finding Your Own North Star: Claiming the Life You Were Meant to Live*, Crown, 2001

Joan Budiliovsky, *The Complete Idiot's Guide to Meditation*, Macmillan, 1998

Dr. Wayne Dyer, *Real Magic: Creating Miracles in Everyday Life*, HarperCollins, 1992

Mark Epstein, *Thoughts Without a Thinker: Psychotherapy from a Buddhist Perspective*, 1995

Shakti Gawain, *The Path of Transformation: How Healing Ourselves can Change the World*, Nataraj, 1993

Tara Bennett-Goleman, *Emotional Alchemy: How the Mind can Heal the Heart*, Harmony Books, 2001

His Holiness the Dalai Lama and Howard C. Cutler, MD, *The Art of Happiness: A Handbook for Living*, Riverhead Books, 1998

Thich Naht Han, *The Miracle of Mindfulness: A Manual on Meditation*, Beacon Press, 1996

Don Miguel Ruiz, *The Four Agreements: A Practical Guide to Personal Freedon*, Amber Allen, 1997

Michael Talbot, *The Holographic Universe*, HarperPerennial, 1992

John Wellwood (ed.), *Ordinary Magic: Everyday Life as Spiritual Path*, Shambala, 1992

Ken Wilbur, *Integral Psychology: Consciousness, Spirit, Psychology, Therapy*, Shambala, 2000; *No Boundary: Eastern and Western Approaches to Personal Growth*, Shambala, 2001

Machaelle Small Wright, *Behaving as if the God in all Things Mattered*, Perelandra, 1997

Feng Shui Resources

FENG SHUI SUPPLIES

www.fastfengshui.com: products and links

Feng Shui Warehouse; 1-800-388-1599; www.fengshuiwarehouse.com

Feng Shui Emporium: 1-800-443-5849; www.fengshuiemporium.com

Petals (life-like plants and flowers): 1-800-920-6000; www.petals.com

FENG SHUI CONSULTANTS

To find a consultant near you, check these on-line directories:

Feng Shui Warehouse: www.fengshuiwarehouse.com

Feng Shui Directory: www.fengshuidirectory.com

Feng Shui Guild: www.fengshuiguild.com

FENG SHUI TRAINING PROGRAMS

These are programs with which I am personally familiar; there are many other fine programs and trainers available.

Contemporary Western feng shui:

The Accelerated Path (Nancy SantoPietro): (718) 256-2640; www.fengshui-santopietro.com

BTB Feng Shui Professional Training Program: (415) 681-1182; www.btbfengshui.org

Interior Alignment (Denise Linn): (808) 239-8878; www.interioralignment.com

The Metropolitan Institute of Interior Design: (516) 845-4033; www.met-design.com

The Western School of Feng Shui (Terah Kathryn Collins): 1-800-300-6785; www.wsfs.com

Traditional Chinese feng shui and astrology:

American Feng Shui Institute (Larry Sang): www.amfengshui.com

Roger Green: www.fengshuiseminars.com

Joseph Yu: www.astro-fengshui.com

Glossary

ba gua A map of the energetic qualities of a space. *Ba gua* means "eight areas"—eight *guas*, or sections, surround a central space, the *tai chi*. Each *gua* has a symbolic association with a specific life aspect or aspiration, such as wealth, career, or relationships, for example. Whatever is going on energetically in each *gua* of your home will affect the related aspect of your life.

Black Sect feng shui A very popular method of feng shui, especially in the U.S., introduced by Professor Thomas Lin Yun. Also called "BTB" (Black Tibetan Buddist) feng shui, this approach aligns the *ba gua* with the entry, rather than to the compass. Black sect feng shui emphasizes the power of intention, and incorporates many "transcendental" cures and rituals.

chi The life force present in all things. The practice of feng shui is based on analysis and correction of the *chi* of a space.

chien The area of the *ba gua* associated with helpful friends and travel. See page 188 for the qualities and location of *chien gua*.

Compass school feng shui A traditional Chinese method of feng shui. Analysis and diagnosis of the feng shui of a building is based on compass orientation and year of construction. More complex and often more difficult to apply than Western feng shui.

Contemporary Western feng shui —feng shui as it is often practiced in America today, with the *ba gua* oriented to the main entry instead of to compass directions. Conscious intention is an important factor in this style of feng shui.

cure An adjustment made with the intention of removing or neutralizing a negative influence or *sha chi*, in order to improve the *chi* of a space. Sometimes also used to refer to feng shui enhancements made to enhance or activate a space, where there is no negative influence to be corrected.

dui   The area of the *ba gua* associated with creativity and children. See page 188 for the qualities and location of *dui gua*.

earth   One of the five elements used in feng shui. See the reference chart on page 203 for a summary of the qualities, shapes, and colors associated with the EARTH element.

empowerment   The process of adding the power of your own intention to your feng shui cures and enhancements. Empowering your feng shui changes with the power of body, speech, and mind is thought to dramatically improve the outcome.

enhancement   An adjustment made with the intention of improving the *chi* of a space. Faceted crystal balls, water fountains and wind chimes are popular feng shui enhancements. Objects and images that have a strong, positive symbolic meaning for the individual are also effective as enhancements.

extension   A part of a room or building that sticks outfrom the rest of the structure and adds strength to that room or *gua*. See page 190 for how to identify any extensions in your home.

Fast Feng Shui[tm]   I created this term to describe my approach to teaching and writing about Contemporary Western feng shui. My emphasis is on: recognizing and working with your feng shui style; targeting your efforts to your individual power spots for maximum results with minimum wasted effort; personalizing the affirmations and visualizations used to empower your changes; the importance of approaching feng shui as tool for change and personal growth.

feng shui   The practice, originally from ancient China, of adjusting the *chi*, or life force, of a space so that the inhabitants experience greater happiness, success, prosperity, and vitality.

fire   One of the five elements used in feng shui. See the reference chart on page 203 for a summary of the qualities, shapes, and colors associated with the FIRE element.

hsun The area of the *ba gua* associated with prosperity and fortunate blessings. See page 188 for the qualities and location of *hsun gua*.

jen The area of the *ba gua* associated with family and health. See page 188 for the qualities and location of *jen gua*.

kan The area of the *ba gua* associated with career. See page 188 for the qualities and location of *kan gua*.

karma The fate that you created for yourself in this life as the result of your actions in past lives; the effect that your current actions will have on your future existence.

ken The area of the *ba gua* associated with self-understanding and spirituality. See page 188 for the qualities and location of *ken gua*.

kun The area of the *ba gua* associated with marriage and relationships. See page 188 for the qualities and location of *kun gua*.

li The area of the *ba gua* associated with fame and reputation. See page 188 for the qualities and location of *li gua*.

mantra A sacred word or phrase used for meditation, prayer, and blessing.

metal One of the five elements used in feng shui. See the reference chart on page 203 for a summary of the qualities, shapes, and colors associated with the METAL element.

missing area A part of a room or building that is indented from the rest of the structure and weakens that room or *gua*. See pages 190-191 for how to identify any missing areas in your home.

power spot A focal point for your feng shui efforts, determined by what life issues you want to address at this time and by the unique qualities and layout of your home. Feng shui becomes easier and more effective when you concentrate on your power spots first, before working on the rest of your home.

red envelopes Feng Shui practitioners of the Black Sect or BTB school follow the tradition of asking for payment to be presented in red envelopes. The red color empowers the client's wishes and provides protection for the practitioner. Red envelopes can also be used to empower a wish or blessing written on a slip of paper and placed in the envelope.

secret arrows *Sha* (negative) *chi* created by sharp objects and angles.

sha chi Harmful *chi* that can cause or aggravate stress, restlessness, and a variety of health problems.

space clearing Specific rituals and other practices designed to remove stale, old, or negative energy from a space.

tai chi The central area of any space, especially the center of your home. Anything going on in the *tai chi* of your home will affect all of the *guas*, so it is a very important area to keep free of clutter and other negative influences.

water One of the five elements used in feng shui. See the reference chart on page 203 for a summary of the qualities, shapes, and colors associated with the WATER element.

wood One of the five elements used in feng shui. See the reference chart on page 203 for a summary of the qualities, shapes, and colors associated with the WOOD element.

Index

Give the gift
of life transformation and personal growth!

additional copies of

$\mathscr{F}$AST FENG SHUI
9 Simple Principles for Transforming Your Life by
Energizing Your Home

and

$\mathscr{F}$AST FENG SHUI *for* SINGLES
108 Ways to Heal Your Home and Attract Romance

can be purchased online at
www.fastfengshui.com
or by calling
1-800-431-1579

Lotus Pond Press
415 Dairy Road, #E-144
Kahului, Maui, HI 96732

Activate your intention with a
Fast Feng Shui "Wish Book"!

A unique and powerful feng shui cure,
created by author and consultant Stephanie Roberts to
beautifully enhance your wishes and intentions!

Each miniature WISH BOOK features hand-marbled or imported paper, satin ribbon ties, instructions card, and paper inserts for recording your intentions. Write your wish on a slip of paper and enclose it in the book, where it is amplified by mirrors inset into the inside covers.

WISH BOOKS are individually hand-crafted in the U.S. in a variety of sizes and designs. They may be placed on a home altar, under your pillow, in a power spot, or carried in a pocket or purse. They make terrific gifts, and may be used to activate any *gua* or intention, from creativity to prosperity to love and romance.

Please visit
fastfengshui.com
ection and ordering information.